DREAMING THROUGH
THE EYES OF GOD

To Joanne,

May God continue to
guide and bless you!

Best Wishes,
Tara Lynn Marta

Dreaming Through the Eyes of God

by

TARA LYNN MARTA

Adelaide Books
New York / Lisbon
2021

DREAMING THROUGH THE EYES OF GOD
By Tara Lynn Marta

Published by Adelaide Books, New York / Lisbon
adelaidebooks.org
Editor-in-Chief
Stevan V. Nikolic

For any information, please address Adelaide Books
at info@adelaidebooks.org
or write to:
Adelaide Books
244 Fifth Ave. Suite D27
New York, NY, 10001

ISBN: 978-1-955196-76-5

Printed in the United States of America

Contents

Introduction

Sometimes amid heartbreak comes healing; a chance to recover from the depths of despair so you can continue God's objective for your life. It can be done. I should know. There was a time when my life was rooted in dejection, when negativity sought to extinguish the light in my soul. Through faith and prayer God took me from obscurity into His loving arms where His plans for my life awaited.

When I lost my father at thirty-two, my entire world imploded. Having lost my mother at twelve, and with no siblings or children of my own, it was the end of my immediate family. For the first time, I felt alone. It was during this low point that anxiety took control, generating a desperate need of renewal.

The power of prayer can change the route of one's life. This I know to be true. After high school, my intentions on attending college were thwarted by a destructive weapon known as fear. Since I had always struggled in academics, I put off college and settled into menial jobs that caused nothing but misery.

All the while my heart ached to write. The written word had been my companion throughout my childhood. Being a writer, however, was a figment of my imagination because I did not have the talent to make my dreams take flight.

Or so I thought.

With my father gone, I was presented with two choices: sink or swim. I had been a quitter in the past, deserting jobs because they were too rigorous; running from college because I did not believe myself smart enough. But I was not about to quit living. While on the treadmill one day, I asked God's intentions for my life. The answer came weeks later when I enrolled in junior college, and again in three years when I went on to a university where I became an English major, and yet again when I turned forty and entered a graduate level Creative Writing program.

Along the way, however, there were minor changes to be made. One of them was allowing God to transform my life. This did not come easily. God had His work cut out for Him. But He kept at me, and each time I failed, He whispered for me to get up, dust myself off, and keep going.

There were other obstacles to defeat before I was strong enough to achieve my dreams, including cutting naysayers out of my life, using fear as a motivator, staying focused on my chosen path, and maintaining my devotion to God in the midst of pain.

God's lessons were not created just for my benefit. They are for anyone who wishes to achieve a dream but lacks discipline. And by achieve I do not mean to suggest that your dreams will come true. At times, the heart of a dream lies not in the actual realization, but in the chain of events during the process.

I am not a psychologist. This book will not solve all your problems. Some issues need professional help (and there is no shame in that). The purpose of this book is to give the dreamer faith-based lessons that helped transform my life and transport me from the couch to a path.

Dreaming is only one half of the mission; using your dreams to honor God is the other.

Life After Loss

When the doctor came into a small waiting area to tell me my father's twenty-year battle with Type 1 Diabetes was over, I cradled my face in my hands and burst into tears. Loss was not new to me. My mother died when I was twelve. Still, grief is not a simple process and losing my father at the age of thirty-two left me unable to cope with the sudden changes in my life.

I was led down a long corridor into a private room where my father's lifeless body lay. Dad's head was titled to the side; his cheek settling against his left shoulder. He had on a white tee-shirt. His face was swollen from the dialysis he had been receiving over the past two months. His coloring was a cross between blue and grey. While his physicality slightly resembled the father I had known, his spirit had departed. I envisioned him sitting up, sipping coffee, and tapping his foot to his favorite music. But he was still.

As I gazed at the man who was once my father, I had mixed emotions. On one hand, he had been set free, no longer imprisoned by a body that had betrayed him since his mid-thirties. On the other hand, what was I going to do without him? I had no siblings or family of my own. My maternal grandmother, whom had been a second mother to me, had died less than a year before. How could I navigate the empty world without them? Without a purpose? I thought about the title of an Elvis song I had once heard: "What now? What next? Where to?"

At one time I was what you would call a "holiday Christian," attending church on Christmas and Easter. God was someone I believed in, even talked to. That did not mean I was willing to hear what He had to say. When He tried to speak to me, I became deaf, dumb, and blind.

Spring 2008: I started going to church on a weekly basis. Something in me began to change; rather than attend mass as a sense of duty, I went on my accord. During one service, I heard a homily that had a profound influence on me. My ears perked up when the priest mentioned the name Emily Dickinson—the famous poet known for her unusual punctuation style and her penchant for depressing themes. The priest spoke about the agony Dickinson suffered after losing her parents. I sat in the back of the church, tugging at my shirt which was too tight thanks to my recent weight gain, astonished that a priest was talking about an iconic literary figure.

As my attention began to drift, the priest said, "When both parents die, they're not really gone. They've simply walked through another door."

At the time his words had little value, however intriguing they may have been. Two weeks after my father died, the sermon tore through my mind. "When both parents die, they're not really gone. They've simply walked through another door."

The Lord works in mysterious ways, and my being in church at the exact time the priest spoke about the loss of both parents was no accident. God wanted to prepare me for a new journey, one without my father.

I had been a motherless daughter for twenty-years but never a total orphan. I felt abandoned when my mother died and anxious when it came to my father's death. Having Dad around meant that I was still his little girl. His passing thrust me into adulthood for the first time.

Parents serve as a barrier. In a strange way, we feel secure knowing that they are the ones standing between us and death's door. That is not to say that kids can't die before their parents, but for those of us who have witnessed the death of both parents, it can be daunting having to step into their shoes—to know that the next person to stand at death's door will be us.

My father's death made me *aware* of my mortality for the first time. There was so much to figure out.

One thing I knew for certain, I could not make it alone.

If anything positive can come from a negative (and it can!), then I believe God led me from grief to my next venture. Nine months after my father walked through the *other door*, I was in a tough spot both physically and emotionally. At 4 ft. 11, my weight totaled 170 pounds—too much for my small frame to withstand. My knees creaked whenever I bent down. I lost my breath if I walked from one room to another. Eating had become a source of comfort, a way to bury my grief. Fast food, ice-cream, potato chips—I used it all to combat stress.

In addition to the weight gain, my morale descended. Immediately following my father's death, I went into a depression. It had been a long road for both me and Dad.

March 1988: My father started losing weight. Though I had no idea what the word diabetes meant, Dad knew he had it, especially when he couldn't stop drinking gallons of water. He went into the hospital for two weeks. My mother and I would eat dinner, then walk downtown to the State Hospital where my father was hooked up to a heart monitor. Doctors rushed in and out checking Dad's sugar, poking him with needles.

One night, I emerged from bed to find my mother lying on the floor in the living room. She had been experiencing abdominal cramping for months, but doctors could not locate the problem, so they misdiagnosed her with an ulcer.

On May 8, 1988, my mother packed her suitcase and called a taxi. "Where are you going?" I asked. Her pain had intensified. She resolved to check herself into the hospital whether doctors agreed or not. She advised my father, who offered to go with her, to wait until she called. Shortly after dinnertime the phone rang. My mother had been admitted. It had been a few weeks since my father came home. Now this. To make matters worse, it was Mother's Day.

After my mother passed away, my father's own hospital visits escalated. Doctors could not seem to control his sugar levels. On the phone with my grandmother one Friday evening, she put me on hold to use the bathroom. I used the opportunity to go down to the kitchen for a snack. To my surprise, I found my father on the floor, slowly slipping into unconsciousness. I ran back to the phone to tell my grandmother. She told me to hang up and call 911.

My fingers raced across the keypad. It seemed an eternity before the operator answered. With the cordless phone in hand, I peeked into the kitchen to see Dad's lanky body still in position.

"The ambulance will be there any minute," the operator explained. She tried calming my nerves with conversation. "How old are you?" *Old enough to wonder what had happened to the carefree days of my childhood.* Whatever normalcy I had ended at twelve-years-old.

It was hard pretending to be a normal teenager with such a heavy burden to bear. Dad's health did not just affect him but me as well. I wanted such simple things, like being able to attend school without fearing that my father wouldn't live long enough to escort me into adulthood.

My second home was the VA Hospital where I spent many hours alone, waiting for news on my father's condition. Sometimes we'd be there until one in the morning or on a holiday.

I envied those who did not have to stop what they were doing to check on a parent, those who never received emergency phone calls at work—like the one I received in 2002. My father wanted to visit my grandmother in Florida. Terrified of flying, he took a bus. He became ill at a bus station in Jacksonville. Thank God for the good soul who saw him safely to a nearby hospital.

The last battle my father faced left him confined to a wheelchair. Once again, he was hospitalized—this time with kidney failure. I was advised by his doctor to place him in a nursing home—something that went against my heart. As I signed the papers, tears gushed down my cheeks.

I have heard it said that the reason people place loved ones in nursing homes is because they do not care about them. Such statements are untrue. My father needed round the clock care, which I could not provide. He stood at 5 ft 8 compared to my 4 ft 11 stature; lifting him was complicated. The nursing home was a last resort.

In between running to hospitals and nursing homes, I developed bronchitis. Suffering a high fever and low blood pressure, I continued to run errands for my father. That is when I wished for siblings the most or for my mother to be alive—someone to assist with the responsibilities on my plate.

I never blamed my father for his unfortunate incidents. Like me, he just wanted to live a normal life.

Trying to figure out life after loss can take time. There is an inclination to give up, to make a run for it. But where do you go? What are the alternatives? It took years before I was able to accept the death of my mother. My father's death left me in an uncomfortable position—alone, afraid.

It is easy to judge others when you have not walked in their shoes. Following my father's death, I am sure there were times when my attitude needed adjustment, times when I seemed aloof or insensitive. I was doing the best I could under new circumstances. I needed to get my footing and learn how to make it without the support of a parent to guide me.

Anytime I had a problem in the past, my parents were there to help me figure it out. If the kids at school made fun of me, my mother would tell me everything would be OK. When co-workers made working conditions difficult, my father would offer advice on how to deal with unruly individuals. Now it was up to me to find my way in the dark.

Church saved me. The gospel began having an impact, and that's when faith intervened.

While on the treadmill in my four-room apartment one afternoon, I thought about the road ahead and posed a question to God—out loud: "Where do I go from here?"

His answer was not what I expected.

"Hear, O' Lord, have mercy on me; Lord, be my helper."
Psalm 30:11

God's Plan

It should be no surprise that God has a trajectory for each of us. Our lives are not our own, so it makes perfect sense that He would create us to carry out specific tasks.

That said, not all of us take the right path. Something known as free will occasionally throws us off course. This happens when we allow distractions such as fear, to get in the way of our chosen path.

The trick is to drown out the noise and listen to God.

If you expect to hear God's voice booming through your home, don't hold your breath. Do not attempt to stand in front of any burning bushes either, because that was reserved for Moses. That does not mean God is not trying to reveal His plan to you. His voice comes in innumerable ways—the conscience, a dream, or another person.

Have you ever asked someone for directions without bothering to follow them? When left to our own devices, we usually end up lost. Free will is a gift that must be used with prudence. Do you have trouble hearing God's voice? Maybe it is time to turn down the volume on the outside racket and tune in to the faint whisper inside your heart.

My mother never believed in coincidence. She felt that God has everything mapped out for us before we even enter the womb. Anytime you find yourself questioning which path to take, ask God for directions. He knows where you are supposed to be and when.

When I asked God to reveal His plan for me, nothing immediate came of it. A few months later I decided to take a walk. I wandered inside the admissions office of the local community college. I had put off higher education after high school for a year, which turned into two, then three, then fourteen. Suddenly, in my thirties, I signed over my life to student loans.

On the way home, I could feel the college catalog bouncing around in my backpack. Three blocks later, my feet came to a standstill. "What just happened?" I thought. I had not set out that day to become an adult learner. It baffled me how such a thing could happen. Recalling my prayer on the treadmill, I realized that God wanted me to go to college because that would eventually lead to my chosen path—writing.

For as long as I can remember, writing has been an integral part of my life. From crayon to pencil to marker—I used them all. I even practiced my autograph on the inside door of my grandmother's medicine cabinet using nail polish. My love of the written word materialized from my devotion to books. As a child, I had every toy imaginable. But nothing compared to the stacks of books strewn around my bedroom. Reading is the gateway to writing. Trying to separate the two is like eating a peanut butter sandwich without the jelly.

When I was old enough, I wrote stories on construction paper, which I then folded to resemble a book. My neighbors would snicker as I went door to door, attempting to sell my masterpiece. I am not sure how many kids self-publish, but it brought me much-needed pocket change for candy.

I received my first beat-up typewriter in 1986, a yellow contraption where my slim fingers jammed between the keys. That's when I turned into a mini-journalist, writing my own version of real stories after seeing them on the evening news.

I never gave writing serious thought. My dream was to be a singer or an actress. Being shy with a poor memory, it was obvious I would never make it in the movies, and the only time I hit a high note was as a baby whenever someone plucked the bottle from my lips.

Somewhere between singing and acting, the writer in me awakened.

God's persistence for me to take writing seriously went ignored. With my will up against His, it took time before I realized that when God set me on course, I veered off track. When that happened, God used my Great-Aunt Anna to try and get His message across.

After sending her one of my fiction stories, Aunt Anna wrote me a letter asking if I had ever considered writing as a career. Being in my early twenties, I hadn't the faintest idea how to become a professional writer. But she persisted, informing me that writing was part of my future—as well as college.

As per my habit, I disregarded my aunt's advice. The notion of being a writer appealed to me, but not the work it entailed. My aunt was convinced that God had given me a clear vision for my future. It was just a matter of when to put His plan into action.

By the time I went to college, my aunt had died. Somewhere she was smiling down saying, "I knew you'd get there."

That did not stop me from feeling like I didn't belong. Due to my age, relating to my classmates was impossible. Everything they did and said was lost on me—lingo, music, parties. At the end of my second semester, I was having serious doubts about whether I belonged in college.

God sensed my inner conflict and put me in contact with a professor who straightened me out. This professor informed me that she had multiple degrees, most of which had been attained mid-life.

God brought me to the right place at the right time. I never again questioned whether I was too old to learn.

My best friend set her mind on being a kindergarten teacher. Within days of her first semester in college, she began feeling dissatisfied in elementary education. Something inside nudged her toward another major. But what? At first, she ignored the whisper and continued to plug away at her coursework.

Out of the blue, she had an overwhelming urge to switch her major to psychology. Teaching children was not what she wanted to do with her life; she wanted to assist children in a different way. She marched over to her advisor's office and changed her major.

Becoming a psychologist meant that she would embark on a ten-year academic journey. Like me, she dealt with her share of naysayers—those who did not see the point of being in school that long. She could have folded, but she stayed with it, discounting what anyone else had to say about her chosen vocation.

When you are in the psychology field, there are three important attributes you need. First, you should be a good listener, someone who absorbs a child's needs and concerns. Children know when you are not being attentive. This leads to the second attribute: empathy. If you can't see things from someone else's vantage point, then you will never be able to understand what they are going through. The third attribute is the ability to remain objective when listening to a child's issues. You cannot assist children when you interject your personal feelings into a session.

God does not make mistakes. When He taps you on the shoulder, turn around. He knew that my friend had a sincere heart, one that could counsel children without judgement. And He was correct. She does not look down on anyone because of their financial or social status. She has a keen awareness that not every child has the same abilities. More importantly, she is genuine, not someone who took a job because the title made her sound important or because of the economic gain.

Is there something you are burning to do? That is a clear indication that God is speaking to your heart. It is the faint whisper of His voice, not yours, that will lead you down the right path. Go to a quiet place and say, "God, help me discover my purpose in this world; reveal my hidden path, and I will do my best to fulfill the destiny you have in store for me. Not mine, but thy will be done."

"Your eyes foresaw my actions; in your book all are written
down; my days were shaped before one came to be."
Psalm 139

19

Naysayers Gonna Nay

Before finishing junior college, I decided that upon graduation I would move on to a university to study English. Unfortunately, the cynics did not partake in my enthusiasm.

Those who attempt to dissuade you from God's plan are known as naysayers.

Because I had waited until my thirties to go to college, it was assumed that I should not waste the experience on an expensive *hobby* like writing. The naysayers insisted that I find a worthwhile career. God, on the other hand, kept telling me to obey my heart.

My parents had always encouraged me to use my own brain. Advice is one thing, control is another. Because I was in a defenseless position when I first started college, I unwillingly changed my major to a more suitable one: Early Childhood Education.

Being a teacher is a noble profession, but like anything else, it must be a calling. It didn't take long for me to realize that being a full-time teacher was not what I wanted to do. Midway through the semester, I changed my major to undeclared. With the stroke of a pen, I freed myself from any obligation concerning a preschool or daycare.

Around this time, I began my first book. Each night I worked furiously at the kitchen table on a novel about a woman living in the past. It was a subject I knew something about since I regularly reverted to my own past—a place that felt safe and familiar.

While working on my novel, I entered some of my short stories in writing contests. And just like wolves the naysayers pounced, making certain that I knew the chances of winning were slim to none. At that point, my spirit disappeared inside an ugly, dark cloud. When it came to my vocation, I allowed the wrong people to steer the ship. I distanced myself from God's voice and tried in earnest to impress others.

Whether you succeed at something is not the point. Never allow others to dictate the odds to you. The fear of losing should not determine the will to try. The only real failure is regret.

By spring 2011, I switched my major again—this time to business. On the first day of Business Finance, I squirmed in my seat, thumbed through the textbook, and all but passed out from panic. Then the professor started laying figures on the whiteboard. Numbers to the left, to the right, up, down, everywhere. Tears welled in my eyes. My spirit had been intended for creative purposes, not finance.

For nine days I continued to be a dutiful student with a *practical* career path. All the while my heart sank. Business can be a lucrative field, but dollar signs mean nothing if you are unhappy.

Each day I sauntered into class knowing the professor was on to me—that she could sense the imposter sitting in the front row, playing the part of a future executive. The image was a hard pill to swallow: me in business attire, a briefcase in one hand, a cup of coffee in the other, trotting to the office where I would engage in the same monotonous routine day in and day out. But I would have a practical career, right? Wrong. A degree in business was not something in which I could abide.

With two semesters left to graduate, I did the unthinkable and took a leave of absence from college.

Frustration drove me to take a semester off. To borrow an obsolete phrase, I was in desperate need to find myself. Or perhaps leaving college was a way to spite the ones who blew out the flame in my heart. For the remainder of the semester, I stayed home and sorted through the differing voices in my head: that of my own, God's, and those whose opinions should not have had any bearing on my life.

Naysayers can complicate things. But they can't do so without your permission. Nobody has the power to make you feel inferior without your consent. I'd like to take credit for that quote, but Eleanor Roosevelt got to it first. Still, she was right.

After months of self-pity, God whispered, "Time to go back." I returned to school determined to get my Associate Degree and be done with college forever. Without writing as a realistic goal, I would not be moving on to a university after all.

As usual, God's master plan prevailed.

Prior to the fall semester, I had signed on as a team leader for freshman orientation. Up until that point, I had never participated in extracurricular activities. I couldn't imagine why God wanted me to give incoming freshmen a guided tour of the campus.

Part of my job as team leader was to take students to the auditorium where they would be treated to a pep talk about the college experience. Once the students settled down, I took a seat in the back where I could close my eyes. After all, the speaker was there for freshman, not seniors. What could he possibly say that would have anything to do with me?

The speaker opened by posing this question: "How many of you expect to make a six-figure salary when you graduate?" Almost every hand shot in the air. The speaker paused momentarily before saying, "There's the door. You can leave." I had nothing to worry about since I didn't have a sensible career plan anyway, so I laid back and tried to doze off. Just as my eyes closed the speaker began to elaborate on his thoughts. This stranger's words poured from his lips to my ears, and I was riveted by what he had to say. Inside that stuffy auditorium on a warm August afternoon, my dreams were reborn.

I learned that this man had dreams when he went to college. Though I cannot recall what he wanted to pursue, it had to do with the arts. His story was much like my own in that he, too, was advised to give up his dreams for a more dependable occupation.

Misery compounded his success because he was not doing what he loved. Then one day he received life-altering news when his doctor informed him that he had cancer. Beyond devastated, he was saddled with regret, the biggest one being that he had not followed his dreams. Despite his cancer going into remission, he cautioned students not to make the same mistake he had. "Life is short," he said. "Sometimes you don't get a second chance."

His words struck a chord with me as I sat in an uncomfortable seat among a flurry of freshman, who did not seem the least bit interested in this man's advice. His message resonated with me on a personal level because my mother was thirty-nine when she died. Whether she had dreams other than being a wife and mother, I will never know. Her plans ended once she was diagnosed with cancer. I did not want to be in the same position one day—to have a doctor look me in the eyes and tell me my time was up.

God had found another way to rekindle my attention. Without the impulse (which was God's whisper) to sign on as team leader, I never would have been in the auditorium to hear such a profound message. As a result, I vowed to further my education by going to a university to earn a B.A. in English.

I thought my days of higher education were over after receiving my degree in 2015. Earlier I mentioned that God speaks to us in numerous ways. He may not send the angel Gabriel to relay the message, but there is always a messenger. It might be a guest speaker with regrets or a great-aunt who believes in your capabilities or a deceased relative in a dream.

For months I weighed the pros and cons of getting a Master's, brooding over what I would study if I ended up going to graduate school. Finally, I prayed for God to guide my decision. He intervened by sending word from a faraway source. My father.

Dad appeared in a dream one night to congratulate me on college. He went on to tell me that I needed to attend graduate school. "No, that's OK, Dad," I said. "I'm done." But my father vowed that more schooling would help accomplish my dream. He waved a book in my face. I noticed that my name and picture were on the back cover.

When I woke up, my first thought was that dead people think everything is so easy. Next, I called a local graduate school for information on their Creative Writing program. A few months later, I added graduate student to my educational resume.

The naysayers continued to question my sanity for taking out additional loans for a degree that offered no promise. But I trusted my father. He told me that if I worked hard, one day, I would write a book.

Perhaps you know a naysayer who is determined to drag your dreams through the mud. Do not be discouraged. God is calling you to do something extraordinary. Had I taken the wrong advice, I would not be writing this book right now. One thing to understand about naysayers, it's not about you. It's about them. Maybe they never had the courage to purse their dreams.

Nobody has the right to interfere with God's plan. Listen to the whisper inside your heart. Or wait for those unexpected hints. Prove the naysayers wrong by working hard for what you want.

Having a dream is a gift, even if you do not know what that dream is just yet. It will come. Be mindful of the signs.

Naysayers gonna nay . . . The only voice that matters is God's.

"Many are the plans in a person's heart, but it is the
Lord's purpose that prevails."
Proverbs 19:21

Fear Is a Good Motivator

A classroom filled with students fresh out of high school did not thrill me, so my first semester of junior college brought much concern. But there was something deeper wracking my nerves. I was aware that when it came to learning, I struggled more than some of my classmates.

Throughout my academic career, I struggled with my studies —math being my biggest drawback. Reading came second. While it may seem strange to think that a future English major had trouble in reading, it is true. Unable to keep up when the teacher assigned passages to read and interpret, I froze. Reading took time; critiquing took even more time. I would stare at the book, hoping the words would register in my mind. All the while my classmates and teacher waited… and waited… and waited.

Studying presented additional challenges. My working memory went into overdrive when recalling facts for tests. Worrying about the SATs during my senior year of high school gave me insomnia. In the end, my scores were so low, no university would have accepted me. I could have gone to junior college, but at the time, my confidence had been severed.

When I finally enrolled in junior college as an adult learner, I took a placement test before being accepted. As predicted, I failed the math section, forcing me to take developmental math.

A light course schedule of three classes was all I could handle. Having been out of school for fourteen years, I did not want to overload my plate. While other students tackled a full course load on top of working, I had to proceed with caution. Learning still took time.

Fast forward to graduate school where my old fear of listening and critiquing reemerged. One of the obligations in the Creative Writing program is to listen to your classmates read, then it is up to each student to critique one other's work. I knew going in that this would be a sensitive area. Even at forty, I could not hear something once and rattle off a detailed analysis.

At one of the mixers—a party where students get acquainted with each another—alumni returned to discuss their experience in the program. Nearly all of them confessed to wanting to quit in the beginning. They stuck with it.

Giving up is always an option, but keep in mind that when you quit something, you will never know your full potential. Challenges are not intended to defeat you. They are hills, sometimes mountains that strengthen you. God does not care how fast you read or whether you can evaluate a poem in an instant. Life is not a race. God does not make it so. We place burdens on one another because we are conditioned by society to be the fastest, the richest, the proudest, the best.

No matter what God calls you to do, He only asks that you not be afraid. He would not bring you to it if He did not think you capable of handling it. All you need is courage.

Do what frightens you. Now that doesn't mean trying something hazardous. But if you are called to a dream, take the risk. Don't run from it because of fear; *do it* because of fear.

By nature, I am a shy person. From kindergarten through senior year, I cringed every time I had to speak in front of classmates. I would crouch down in my seat whenever the teacher asked for volunteers to answer a question. But teachers have a nose for fear; they sniff it out like a hound. Sure enough, I was always called on. My fear of speaking was so debilitating, I would shake violently, my voice cracking mid-sentence.

Being a writer seemed ideal. I could hide behind a computer screen in my pajamas. A solitary lifestyle suited me. I failed to realize that writers market their work by doing readings.

God will often place you in situations where your stamina is tested. In the Creative Writing program, we had to do our capstones in front of a large audience made up of our peers, professors, and anyone from the public willing to attend. The idea of facing strangers horrified me. When it was my turn, I dug my nails into the wooden lectern. My knees wobbled; my chin trembled. After it was over, I breathed a sigh of relief, telling myself that I would never again endure such an ordeal.

The more I scoffed at the idea of public speaking the more God made me do it, until the time came when I *volunteered* to read my work. While searching for writer's groups on Facebook one afternoon, I came upon an advertisement for a local Writers' Showcase. I attended and introduced myself to the host. After getting acquainted, I asked if I could read one of my published short stories at the next showcase. It took amazing courage to volunteer for a public reading. It also took the hand of God to push me.

By trusting God, I overpowered my fear. Notice I said overpower not eliminate. My insides still quiver when I speak in public. But fear no longer holds me back.

When you find yourself ready to run from a challenge, stop. Step up to the plate and take the bat. God doesn't want you to be afraid. He is at your side always. Trust Him. I'm sure when Elizabeth found out she was going to bear a child in her old age, she thought about running for the hills. Zechariah's disbelief caused his voice to cease until he was ready to trust God's will. A fourteen-year-old Mary had every reason to be skeptical when she was informed by an angel that she would bear the son of God. Even Joseph had to summon faith when he agreed to be Jesus's father.

Trust is an important factor in conquering fear. The enemy knows this, which is why he tries to deter you. Had I not trusted God, I never would have entered college in my thirties, grad school in my forties, nor went on to become a writer. I might not have volunteered to do public readings. My fear would have prevented my first book from being published had I listened to the world's negativity.

The Lord lays the foundation to your dreams. He then provides tools. But it's up to you to build your dreams into a reality. God will take you where you need to go once you put fear aside.

"Do not be afraid; do not be discouraged, for the Lord
your God will be with you wherever you go."
Joshua 1:9

The Need for Greed

Many in our culture are led by the wrong almighty—the dollar. As a writer you will not see any money for a long time. In fact, if your heart is set on a life in the arts, you may never see a penny. Do you throw in the towel? Absolutely not! When you love something from the depths of your soul, keep at it. Jump the hurdles, sidestep the obstacles, and overcome the rejections, because you are dedicated not to money but to a vision.

Don't misunderstand, you need income to survive. Do whatever it takes to pay bills while keeping the dream alive.

When I received my M.A., although it was not in education, I was able to substitute teach grades K-12. I had dropped out of the education program in junior college because teaching was not my dream job. Subbing was something I could do temporarily to pay bills. Also, God had opened a door for me. When the Lord opens a door, it's not wise to slam it in His face.

I have always believed that there is a difference between a job, a career, and a dream. You take any job necessary to pay bills—like it or not. You choose a career by getting a degree in a specific area so you can pay bills. Dreams are what you work toward in between jobs and careers.

In 2016, I received an email informing me that one of my short stories had been accepted for publication. I told anyone who would listen about the good news. Sure enough, my good cheer was met by the annoying question, "Are you getting paid?" The answer of course was no. Faces dropped; smiles disappeared. What a way to dampen the mood!

Dreams require sacrifice. This is notably true in the arts. Though my publication did not bring income, it put my name on the map as a writer.

I feel sorry for people whose happiness solely involves money. They have no concept of the elation that comes from fostering a dream. Net-worth should never determine self-worth. It's wonderful to be paid to do something you love. It's also OK to dream for free, too.

The need for greed can cause unfair judgement. My parents fought to make ends meet throughout their marriage. They worked but still had trouble staying afloat. After they died, others felt the need to rehash their struggles. We never owned a house or a car or took vacations. Funny how I never noticed until people pointed it out.

Memories of my parents do not come with a price tag. I recall going for walks, listening to my father's records, watching television, and playing board games. We did not have much money could buy, but we had each other.

Having money does not free you from stress. Even people without financial worries find themselves inundated with problems because they have replaced faith with money.

Needing money to live is not a vice but replacing God with the love of money is. You cannot serve two masters. Should you get rid of your house and burn all your money? Of course not. Just do not allow it to consume your heart. Or better still, your common sense.

Casting condemnation on someone because they don't have expensive toys should make you reevaluate your standards. My father had a saying: "You can't take it with you." In death, you leave this world with exactly what you came into it with—your soul. Is it not a pity, then, to put so much emphasis on materialistic items?

Those blessed with abundance always need to upgrade. If they have a nice home, they want a bigger one. If they drive a simple car, they want something with the latest gadgets. If they have money, it is never enough. Lack of satisfaction is like saying to God, "I know you have blessed me with much but give me more." In some cases, a bigger home is necessary if you have a family and require extra space. But overindulging can be gluttonous.

Shortly after my father died, an unfortunate incident occurred. In the basement of my apartment building was a storage room where I had some of my parents' belongings. They were not worth much, but to me the items were priceless. After neglecting to lock the door, a thief broke in and stole everything.

Barricaded inside my bedroom, I sulked for days. It was as if my parents had died all over again. But wait! Their souls were free from earthly possessions. In my subconscious, I convinced myself that my parents' belongings somehow kept them alive. A trip to the cemetery cured me when I stared down at the cold, granite stones bearing their names. Nothing they had owned would bring them back. One thing the thieves did not take, though, were my memories.

The association of material items with a person is natural. However, nothing can replace a loved one. You don't need anything except a heart to feel their presence. When you are lonely, don't search for something that once belonged to that person. Go to God instead. Ask Him to keep your loved ones close. Then talk to them. Yes, out loud. Why not?

No one knows how long they have in this world. Do not squander your time fretting over materialistic items. More importantly, resist judging others over them. Remember, you can't take it with you. No amount of money can buy you happiness. And it certainly won't buy back your soul.

"For the love of money is the root of all evil, and some people in their desire for it have strayed from the faith and have pierced themselves with many pains."
1 Timothy 6:10

Remain Focused

Have you ever noticed a horse wearing blinders? They wear these to prevent distractions. That's what you need to do when God offers you a dream. Only don't use real blinders or you'll be locked up. Use imaginary ones.

Staying focused requires diligence. How many times have you revisited past situations that caused you aggravation? We can all plead guilty to that offense at one time or another. Being submerged in sufferings will slow down the process of transformation. It will drain your energy until you can no longer facilitate God's vision.

At one time, I surrendered to negativity, allowing the wrong thoughts to control my mind, which in turn affected my health. When that happened, everything else stopped. The physical impact of my detrimental thoughts triggered constant headaches, nausea, and anxiety.

Residing in anger will confuse your body, which cannot tell the difference between past and present. Therefore, your body will react as if the incident is taking place now, causing unwanted health issues.

My grandmother used to love to say, "Give it to God." You may feel compelled to do battle with a nemesis, to give as good as you get, but you will reap the consequences. Anger takes a lot of energy, not to mention time. Rehashing something that happened ten years ago is time you will never get back. And trust me, the other person likely does not even know you are angry with them.

It took time to understand what my grandmother meant by "give it to God." We are conditioned by society to believe that if anyone hurts us, we should return the favor. That is not how God created us to be. You may be asking, "What about an eye for an eye?" Punishments will be done according to the Lord. We are called by God to forgive, not so much for the other person, but for ourselves. Forgiveness allows us to move on.

One afternoon I was riding the bus after a long day of work when a group of teenagers boarded. They began using profanity. I looked over and silently alerted them of their inappropriate language. One of the young men met my stare with a derogatory comment. Without self-control I would have resorted to name calling, thereby lowering my standards to that of an adolescent. Instead, I prayed that God would soften the boy's heart. The next time I took the bus the same boy got on. Upon seeing me, he put down his head.

The first time I taught a class, my voice shrieked like Mickey Mouse. The kids doodled in their notebooks, some put their heads on the desk and fell asleep. I went home disappointed. Why had God made me a substitute teacher when it clearly wasn't my forte? And yes, I wanted to quit. Something inside, however, would not allow it. I had run from challenges for too long, concealed beneath a shroud of insecurity. So, every morning during prayers, I asked God to give me strength to get through the day. Then I asked that He reveal the reason why I was a substitute teacher.

The answer came when a student complimented me on my teaching. Because I had struggled in school, God knew that I could relate to students who had difficulties in certain areas. It was humbling when kids told me they understood something because of my teaching methods. Some kids knew that I loved to read. The minute they walked into class, they pulled out their favorite books to show me. Inspiring a student is by far one of the most rewarding experiences. It was not long until teaching became second nature.

As usual, there was a lesson attached to being a substitute teacher—to broaden my comfort level in another field God had in store for me—that of a speaker.

I do not recall choosing to become a speaker. It was not on my bucket list, but it was on God's. I found this out after being invited to speak at my former college about my journey as a writer. This was new domain for me, so it seemed. When students filed into the library, my initial reaction was one of terror, until I beseeched God to show me the way.

The substitute teacher then formed into the public speaker. My stiff stance relaxed, letting me move about the room with ease, where I was besieged by curious minds eager to learn what a career in writing was like. Had the Lord not called me to teach, I never would have been comfortable as a guest speaker.

Every door that opens is a new opportunity. It is vital not to question God's plans or to allow others to distract you. You will never know if you can do something unless you give it a shot. Put on your blinders and remain focused.

"Let your eyes look directly forward and
your gaze be straight before you."
Proverbs 4:25

Transforming into a Better You

The Lord called me to enter college to better myself. Education helped me to grow intellectually by attaining critical reading and thinking skills. But it would require spiritual growth to abolish harmful behaviors that sought to defeat God's intent for my life.

To transform into a better you, discard your former self in exchange for the person God designed you to be. If the Lord provides you with a dream, you cannot achieve that goal while demonstrating deeds that will endanger your soul.

Serious corruptions will cause you to stray from God, as well as cheat you out of your dreams. The enemy aims to destroy our spirit, causing us to fall prey to his deceptions.

Have you ever wondered why some people lose everything? Why they seem bent on wasting God's talent? Many individuals end up meeting an early demise due to perilous conduct (think in terms of celebrities). The answer may be one of faith, or lack thereof.

Success is seductive; it offers a wide variety of temptations to direct attention away from God. When the mind is employed by depravities, dreams will falter. Whether it is a Grammy Award winning voice or an Academy Award performance, talent is gifted by God. As such, it should be treated sensibly. Knowing who you are in the eyes of God will keep you from giving in to temptation.

You do not have to be famous to lose your soul or to wreck your dreams. We are all capable of making poor choices. Handle God's inspiration with care. You will not execute your dreams without proper alteration of your inner self.

Anger is perhaps the biggest culprit in destroying us from the inside out. Each of us is put to the test daily. Someone does or says something we do not like, and we fly off the handle.

Once I began attending church more, I noticed the hypocrite staring back at me in the mirror. God had given me a path to a new life—one that required diligence, perseverance, and conversion. But without a willingness to conform to His ways, the mountain I faced would have been impossible to climb.

You may think it is unattainable to be a good Christian all the time, and you would be correct. We are sinners, but that's not an excuse to live in ignorance. When you commit to the Lord, you are pledging to follow His example. Atone for your mistakes. *"Go and sin no more,"* Jesus said. Life cannot be lived without error. It can be lived without repetition of the same error.

I have always considered the world a university. Failing does not mean you should give up. Improving oneself is what being a Christian is all about.

Are you prone to name-calling when you disagree with someone? Resist saying something that cannot be taken back. Labels such as "idiot," "stupid," or worse, are forms of bullying. Consider the emotional cost of harmful words. Verbal abuse will cause the victim to become insecure. The victim could then turn into the abuser by targeting someone else.

Think before you act. When you say anything that causes emotional injury, make amends by acknowledging your error. Words are like arrows that shoot straight through the heart of another. They can be uplifting or demoralizing. Building confidence is a better option than destroying it. WWJD?

It's been said that although we are made in God's image, we are not God. In other words, we cannot help what we do because we're human. If you live by this notion, then the enemy has won. Each day is a blank page, a new beginning. Do not be tempted to relive your blunders. Start writing a new narrative on that blank page.

Do you know someone with the same disposition in their sixties that they had in their twenties? That is because they refuse to grow spiritually. Have you ever heard anyone use their age as reason not to change? "I'm old and there's nothing I need to learn." Whether you are twenty, thirty, or fifty—it is just a number. Age without development denotes nothing. In the words of the great American writer Isaac Asimov: "Education is not something you can finish."

When you step into today, leave the old you in the past. There will always be something to improve. Evolving does not end; it will continue until the last breath is drawn.

It takes courage to recognize that we are indeed fallible. Taking time to analyze oneself does not come as easily as criticizing someone else's faults. Better yourself by pinpointing where modifications are needed. Dig deep within the layers of your soul until you locate the areas in need of transformation. Then begin the process.

I knew that I could not tackle my dreams without shedding some skin. Anger, pessimism, callousness—all had to be eradicated so I could become a better person. Toxic behavior is counterproductive.

Being a Christian is more than a title, it requires action. It is not enough to attend church on Sunday if you leave the gospel behind as soon as you reach the parking lot. Apply it to your way of living.

Transform into a better you so that the dreams God has in store will not be disrupted by the wicked ways of the world.

I cannot call myself a writer if I don't practice my craft. Title alone is not enough. The same goes for Christianity. Walking in your own footsteps rather than in Jesus' will take you the wrong way.

"Do not be conformed to this world, but be transformed by the renewal of your mind, that by testing you may discern what is the will of God, what is good and acceptable and perfect."
Romans 12:2

Look Inward

We tend to believe that God has to grant our every wish. When that wish goes unfulfilled, we play the blame game. Faith in this scenario is used to get what we want.

Although I lost my mother when I was twelve and had a father suffering from diabetes, there was never a time when I blamed God. Sure, I wondered why my mother had to die so young, and why my remaining parent couldn't have better health. But I never lashed out at God.

While many Christians take time to thank God for their blessings, others lose faith at the first sign of trouble. This happened to a woman I knew. For years she quoted the Bible, wore a crucifix, and went to church. Through the years, something changed. Her Christian values deteriorated. Anger replaced compassion. Spite replaced kindness. Selfishness replaced generosity. If a man broke up with her, it was God's fault. Day by day rage flourished until there was nothing left of her Christian nature.

This person only knew God when they got their way. Her loss of faith was a result of unfulfilled dreams and failed relationships. When God did not approve her requests, He went from being a teammate to a rival.

The woman's love was possessive. Her rituals included spying on boyfriends, calling them repeatedly when they did not call her on time, insisting they were cheating on her, etc. She did not know how to give without taking. God's plea for her to come down off her pedestal went unheard. She held Him accountable for her adversities.

Ninety-nine percent of our troubles are self-inflicted. We choose to be self-destructive or to allow others to take us down. If there is something about your life that isn't right, change it. There is nothing wrong with seeking help, either. Talk to a priest, pastor, nun, psychologist—someone who can assist in your transformation. You've heard the expression if something isn't broken, don't try to fix it? Now reword that sentence to read if something is broken, fix it.

God will make you face a problem until you are strong enough to overpower it. In my youth, my mother could not go into another room without me shadowing. After she died, I felt lost, searching for the next person to latch onto. Each time I tightened my grip, the person slipped through the cracks of my fingers.

God was telling me that while there is nothing wrong with having close relationships, they can stifle your progression if you become too dependent. That is what happened to me. I got so wrapped up in others that I abandoned my own responsibilities.

No one enjoys physical or emotional pain, but on occasion, we need to get knocked down to stand up straight. Suffering creates dependence on God by reminding us that we need someone bigger than ourselves to survive.

Who would have thought that anything positive could come from my father's death? God saw my misery and waited for me to ask for His supervision. He then gave me a new life. It is unlikely that I would have gone to college had my father lived. The sting of his death caused me to pursue a new direction. Pain leads to survival, survival adds to strength, and strength turns into wisdom.

Your dreams may not be fulfilled right away. Take a second to consider that not everything works according to *our* time-table. Sometimes God waits. When the time is right, He will deliver. If not, maybe He is waiting for you to work on something in your life before you carry out His will.

Close your eyes and pray. Analyze what you need to change about yourself to make life more compatible. Blaming God is an excuse to deflect responsibility away from yourself. Accept what you cannot change, change what you can. If you want to finger point, look inward not upward.

"Affliction produces endurance, and endurance produces character, and character produces hope."
Romans 5:3

Spending Time with God

A few summers ago, I attended a religious pilgrimage. While in line to receive communion, the woman behind me remarked, "This needs to be over." Her reaction stupefied me. Why was she in attendance if her heart was not in it? Being present in form but not in spirit does not win you bonus points with God. Your time with Him should be at the top of your list.

As a kid, I dragged my feet to church. Children prefer to play not pray. My enthusiasm for church emerged in my twenties and again in my thirties when my actual transformation began.

Every Sunday I enjoy a certain routine: I drive to Dunkin Donuts, order a breakfast sandwich and tea, then park near the church, and turn on Christian music, while enjoying a peaceful prelude to mass.

All of us have people whose company we relish. We choose to engage with that person by spending time with them. It is incumbent upon all who follow God to do so willingly. If you find church tedious or have zero time to devote to your maker, then you need a transformation.

Church should not have the same negative effect that an unexciting place of employment does. Some of us hate our jobs for different reasons. Going to church should not be in the same category as a dull job. Go to the Lord with open arms. If you cannot devote time to God, how can you be dedicated to your dreams?

If I wasn't praying the day I asked for God's intercession, my dream would have gone unrealized. His guidance directed me to the admission's office of the local college. The rest is history.

Can you get to a destination without first checking a map? How about when you want to cook a new dish? You need a recipe before you add ingredients. We consult doctors, lawyers, instruction manuals. Doesn't it make sense to consult God about our dreams?

Listening to God empowered me to make wise decisions which took me from a dream to a classroom to being published. It is when you make time for the Lord that He will begin to reveal strategies to get you on the right path.

Before God became a prominent fixture in my prayer life, I made terrible decisions. The first was not going to college right away. The second was not believing in my dreams. My third and worst decision was taking life for granted.

Drifting through the twenties is not out of the ordinary because you are still trying to figure things out. That said, had I spent more time with God in those early years, I might not have withered away an entire decade being miserable. Although I ended up going to college, it is important to note that tomorrow is not promised.

When you accept the Lord into your life the upshot should be pleasure. He is comfort, joy, satisfaction. Avoiding Him will prolong your transformation. Offer yourself fully to the Lord. You need to be present in mind, body, and spirit. And without complaints.

"He who dwells in the shelter of the Most High
will rest in the shadow of the Almighty."
Psalm 91:1

Maintaining a Relationship with God

It is relevant to maintain a relationship with God. Imagine not talking to your spouse for weeks at a time. Or walking around the house ignoring your kids. Relationships cannot survive without interaction. Why should your relationship with God be any different?

Because we cannot see or hear Him, we can forget He's there. That is why it is imperative to seek Him throughout the day.

There was a time when I was too busy to call on God. If He heard from me, it was because of a problem that required His attention. During my transformation, however, I found myself reading the Bible more and doing daily devotionals. Through the years I have amassed several devotional books to guide me in my spiritual journey.

The first thing I do every morning is pray. I make a cup of tea, gather my devotional books, and meditate. To help assist in my relationship with God, I keep two journals. One is to write down my favorite Bible verses. The other I refer to as my "God journal," where I jot down my thoughts and prayers. I begin every journal entry with "Dear God." This allows me to engage in full conversation with the Lord. Then I tell Him what's on my mind, whether it is something I am grateful for or troubled by. Nothing is off limits with God. By doing this, I am actively pursuing my maker. Without His presence, life cannot flourish.

When someone dies, you think of them regularly. You reminisce by looking at photographs, watching videos. Though you cannot see nor hear them, they are a constant in your life. This is because you want to keep them close. Do the same with God. Talk to Him. Meditate on His word. Go to church.

When I lived in Brooklyn, I made friends in kindergarten. We played together, went over one another's houses, and called each other on the phone, until my family uprooted to Pennsylvania in 1985. For a short time, I continued to keep in touch with my friends through letter writing. Once or twice their parents brought them for a visit. As time wore on, we grew apart. The letters stopped. So did the visits.

You cannot expect to maintain a relationship with God without contacting Him. But don't expect the Lord to intrude on your time. Have you ever seen the famous painting of Jesus knocking outside a door? Missing on the door is the knob. This is to remind us that Jesus will not enter until we invite Him in.

Many of us enjoy some form of exercise each morning, whether it is going to the gym, for a run, or doing Pilates. Our bodies respond to exercise because such activities strengthen our muscles. Imagine the soul as a muscle. It needs activity from God. Saying prayers is like lifting weights. Each prayer reinforces your soul by making it stronger and healthier.

While in college, I stopped checking in with God for a bit. Overwhelmed by schoolwork, naysayers nipping at my nose, and the loss of my father all took its toll. Once that happened, I stopped growing, as did my dreams. My temper increased while my morals decreased. This led to a lack of self-control over my words, actions, and emotions.

With my defenses lowered the enemy stepped in. I did not feel good enough to be a child of God, nor well-suited to accept the dreams God had given me. The farther away from God I got, the closer the enemy came to destroying my life.

When you find yourself harboring negative thoughts, be mindful of the one putting them in your head. The enemy comes to steal your glory, to drain your energy, to twist your thoughts, to manipulate your mind. The parasite making you feel worthless can be defeated by God. Turn to Him in times of trouble. He will lead you from pain to renewal.

My father's death was a turning point in my life. I would never have reached my goals without an *internal restoration*, aka a cleansing of the soul. God transformed me from the inside out. In the process, I overcame many of my demons, but this only came to be because of my continual relationship with God.

We have all defied a higher authority—parent, teacher—anyone looking out for our greater good. Having self-control terrifies the sinner. It is much easier to spew profanity than it is to control your mouth. It is easier to punch the wall than to step back. Anger seeks quick relief. But if you are prone to cheap methods, then you suffer from a lack of self-control. One of the ways to stay in control is to remember to whom you belong. Be observant in how you choose to conduct yourself.

As an Italian, I know firsthand about losing my temper. In a fit of rage, our first instinct is to strike back. That is when you ask God for governance. Remember in the Bible when Jesus instructed Peter to put away his sword? It is because those who live by the sword die by the sword. Walking away from a fight is not weak. Standing up to someone requires strength but not the kind that leads to physical confrontation. It takes more courage to work something out rationally than it does to demonstrate vengeance.

When you arrive at a situation that tests your patience, remember that you are not your own. You have been bought and paid for by the Lord. Stay strong by having God present all day, every day. Prayer leads to power.

A relationship cannot thrive without effort. You can't know yourself—or your dreams—unless you know God. The Lord is ready to give when you are willing to make time for Him.

"Behold, I stand at the door and knock. If anyone
hears my voice and opens the door, I will enter his
house and dine with him and He with me."
Revelations 3:20

The Heart of a Dream

Having a dream does not ensure success. Some of us dream of becoming a celebrated singer, artist, or athlete. Just because God gives you a passion for something does not guarantee that you will be the next Dolly Parton, Monet, or Babe Ruth. It does not mean you should give up, either. If you are seeking fame, you are dreaming for the wrong reasons.

Every writer fantasizes about publishing a best-seller so they can sip green tea beside Oprah while discussing their latest tome. But fame is not the conquest to having a dream, nor is being rich. A dream means fulfilling your obligation to the Lord.

When my first fiction story was published in an online literary journal, I cried tears of joy. It did not make me well-known. To be honest, no one probably even read it. I am a writer because I was granted a love for storytelling, not because I expect to be the next Willa Cather.

Everything you do should be done for the glory of God. While dreams may appear to stem from our own interests, it is God who has granted us the skills we possess. We are obligated to honor the Lord by fulfilling His purpose. That purpose may not include reaching the finish line, but the expedition will not be in vain.

We are lured to the culture's impression of how we are to live. From the time we are born those presumptions come in many forms: marriage, a house with a white picket fence, a new car, a high-paying job, etc. But what if you stay single, live in an apartment, drive a used car, or have a job that just about pays the bills? Society says that you are not worthy unless you conform to its criteria.

The heart of a dream is not about how much money you make or whether your name ends up in lights. God expects nothing less than pure joy. If you are a writer, joy is in the art of writing. Nowhere does the Lord say you have to win the Pulitzer.

Do what God has instructed without expecting financial gain or honorary distinction. You may want economic stability: stocks, bonds, a comfortable pension, but unless your heart is satisfied, none of it will matter. When you approach the end of your life, the last thing you want to think about is could have, would have, should have.

All dreams bear God's thumbprint. Doctors should not study medicine because of the sports cars they will be able to afford. The goal should be to honor God by treating the sick. Firefighters honor God by extinguishing fires that threaten the lives of others. In law enforcement, your priority is to honor God by upholding the law. Do you wish to get married? Have kids? You will honor God by being faithful to your spouse and instilling good values in your children.

At the very core of your dreams should be the desire to please God. In this form of Thanksgiving, you are showing Him that you will use His generous offerings to benefit those around you.

My first novel dealt with the inability to cope with loss. God wanted me to write about loss because it is such a universal topic, something each of us must endure. I wrote my novel so that readers would see in the protagonist their own pain and learn how to survive. By doing this, I spread God's message that those we love remain part of us.

What happens when you put your blood, sweat, and tears into a dream that does not pay off? Keep going. Nothing that comes from God is a failure. Dreams are not measured by a pass/fail standard. All God asks is that we do the best we can. No one is going to mark you unsatisfactory if you do not grab the brass ring. Love what you do with all your heart.

You do not have to excel at everything. My second career choice would have been to paint beautiful canvases like my favorite artist, Vincent van Gogh. Unfortunately, I was not given the talent to perfect a stick figure much less paint exquisite landscapes. Who says you can't enjoy something unless you master it?

I love a good game of tennis. Yet I spend more time hitting my shins than the ball. Being a poor tennis player does not stop me from playing. The sheer pleasure of being on a tennis court is enough.

The heart of a dream can be about the experiences you have with other dreamers. I relished striking up friendships with fellow writers that I met doing speaking engagements. After one of my essays was published in an anthology, I, along with additional contributing writers, set out on a mini book tour. We did readings in bookstores, cafes, college campuses, etc. There was something so empowering about a group of women writers coming together to share their personal stories through poetry, essays, artwork, and prose.

At the book launch, we autographed books, ate cake, posed for photos. The attention we received was nice, but nothing compared to the excitement of having our words touch so many readers.

The anthology gave me the chance to work with incredible writers. Had I not taken the time to submit my work, I would never have met likeminded writers who shared my love for the written word.

Bear in mind, however, your identity is not your dream. It is not that of brother or sister, mother or father, husband or wife. It is not that of a failure. You came into the world a child of God. That is who you will be when you leave here.

I am not concerned with the number of books I sell or whether they end up best-sellers. If my words can touch the heart of one person, then I have honored God by using His gift for the right purpose.

Use your gifts to inspire and delight. And never forget—a true dream exceeds prestige and wealth.

"I have spared you to show you my power and to make my name resound throughout the earth."
Exodus 9:16

Letting Go

Following a dream is not easy when harboring pain. Letting go is one the greatest undertakings. When it comes to loss, we tend to believe that letting go means forgetting those we love.

I had just turned twelve when my mother was diagnosed with pancreatic cancer. From the moment of diagnosis her fate was sealed. The doctor gave her six months to live; she lasted a little more than a month. It is hard to process the death of a parent—for a child, even more so. The woman I had trailed around the house, the one who could not go anywhere without me pitching a fit, disappeared from my life.

Adolescence transitions us from childhood into adulthood. My progression was slow-moving. My mother's death haunted me. I refused to visit the cemetery because that was confirmation that she was not coming home. I had my father box up her clothes and put them in the attic. No photos of my mother existed in my bedroom, either.

The only realization of my mother's death was a quote I cut out of a magazine and taped to my wall. It read: "Mom, where did you go. I had plans."

In school, teachers wrote notes to my father informing him of my disastrous grades. When I'd get sick and be sent to the nurse, she would ask if I wanted to call my mother. "No," I'd say, "she's too busy. Call my father."

Nothing mattered to me anymore—not school, family, or friends.

By twenty, I was still holding on to yesterday until my Great-Aunt Anna presented me with a challenge. In a phone conversation, she told me that I needed to "give my mother to God." At first her declaration astonished me. Give my mother to God? But I already had.

We sometimes believe that we are entitled to possess others, to retain them even after they have long gone. My grief prohibited my mother from being set free. She remained confined to a time and place she no longer belonged, all because I denied the fact that although she carried me in her womb, she did not belong to me.

By 2008, I had lost my father, maternal grandmother, and two aunts—all of whom had been close to my heart. Letting go of a loved one is the hardest thing to do; holding on is even harder.

My parents' deaths played in my mind like an old movie. I thought of waking up on that Sunday morning in June to find my mother gone. I knew the day was coming; still, I was unprepared. Days before, I sat on the floor while my mother rested on the couch. "Mom," I said, "when you get to heaven, will you ask God if you can visit me once in a while?"

After she was gone, I wrote a letter to God asking if I could see her one more time. I buried the note in the backyard. Obviously, I never saw my mother again, though I am convinced that I heard her calling my name one day and took that as a sign that although I could not see her, she was still with me.

One Sunday morning in April, my father's doctor called me into a private room to tell me he passed away. Months later,

I was on a bus trip, gazing out the window as the world rushed by. All I could hear were the doctor's words: "He passed away. He passed away. He passed away."

Emotions run high with loss. Some of us experience regret: things we should have said or should not have said; things we should have done or should not have done. We try to bargain with God hoping for a miracle that will send a loved one back to us. We experience denial. For years I tried to convince myself that my mother was on vacation. I'd run home from school hoping she'd be back.

There is a high cost to being stuck in grief. My years as a teenager were wrought with anger, bitterness, and sadness. While I did manage to enjoy certain aspects, much of my life passed me by. The same thing happened when my father died. For a while, my safe zone was the couch. I rarely had enough vigor to write, leaving my dreams to hang in the balance.

In the end, acceptance is the only option. Just as I had with my mother, I had to give my father back to God.

God did not place me on this earth just to be the daughter of Barbara and Michael. I will always love and miss my parents. But as a child of God, I have my own road to walk. My job will not be complete until He calls me home.

We will be reunited with our loved ones when the time is right. Until then, there is work to be done and dreams to be dreamed.

"We do not want you to be unaware, brothers, about those who have fallen asleep, so that you may not grieve like the rest, who have no hope. For if we believe that Jesus died and rose, so too will God, through Jesus, bring with him those who have fallen asleep."
1 Thessalonians 4:13-14

Testing the Waters

One of life's essential questions is why humans are made to suffer. The reason for this is because, like Peter, we are being tested. As followers of Christ, we can expect an arduous journey. Whether our trials be familial, financial, or social, we can be sure of one thing—if we divert our eyes away from the Lord, we will sink. Therefore, we must get through our troubles by trusting God to keep us afloat.

How often have you rejoiced in the Lord when things are going right, but the moment life deals you a terrible hand, you lose interest? In moments of desperation, we are quick to allow the enemy to destroy our serenity.

But take heart! Beyond the storm is God's hand. Take it and He will pull you to shore. All you need is faith. Keep your eyes on the one who calms the sea, not the one who rocks the boat.

There are times when children do things they shouldn't. Parents send them to their rooms until they learn their lesson. This is commonly referred to as a punishment, but a better term would be a test. Most kids will stomp their feet in a huff, yet they continue to depend on their parents, because even a child knows that they cannot make it in the world without a wiser hand. Think of God the same way. You will require His leadership regardless of how many times He tests your will.

I dreaded having to take college math. Numbers have never been my strong suit. In order to graduate, I had to complete several math courses. On the first day of Algebra, the professor stood in front of the class and started reading from the textbook. It was like she was speaking another language. While she threw figures on the whiteboard, sweat streaked down my face. It was all so complex, so beyond my comprehension. Just as expected, I failed the first test. Then I failed the second test. The professor noticed my distress and approached me. "I can see you're having difficulty with this course," she said. "Don't give up." I ended up passing the course with a solid C. The lesson, however, had nothing to do with math. It was all about perseverance. Life's tests will never end. You may not understand the reason for the examinations, but trust that God knows what He is doing. Endurance is a strong attribute, one that requires you to put pride aside.

I have known writers who chose to disengage from their art simply because things did not work out at first try. They were under the impression that a *Fairy Godwriter* would turn them into professional writers instantly. Never did they stop to consider that God was testing their will. They gave up without effort.

I knew a woman who wanted to sing. Her dream was to perform in a talent show, and, hopefully, win. She never did. Though *she* was not discouraged, pesky naysayers advised her to give up singing. "You tried, now it's over," she was told. Really? Imagine if Elvis Presley had given up, or Judy Garland, or any other dreamer who dealt with rejection. Thankfully, this woman is still singing even if she never earns a gold record. If God is testing her will, then she is surely passing the test.

As a dreamer, you will be tested. Many times, I questioned if I'd make it as an author. There were days when I felt on top of my game, and days when I wanted to fling my notebook across the room. God wants to know how serious you are about your dreams. The way to show Him is to keep working hard. If you are an actor, take every part you can get. If you are an artist, paint anything you see. Do you dream of running a marathon? Then train by running all the time. On slow days when nothing seems to be going right—be still. Wait. Listen. Learn. Then go.

Even though fear is a natural component to being human, all you need is the faith of a mustard seed to pull you through.

God is testing your spirit to see how far you are willing to go, how hard you are willing to fight. When it rains, believe that the rainbow will soon appear. When you lose a job, trust that you will find another one. When a loved one dies, know that they have gone home. When you have a dream, don't be deterred by occasional roadblocks.

Have faith and keep taking the test.

"Why are you terrified, O you of little faith?"
Matthew 8

The Child Within

As a substitute teacher I have learned one thing from children—
they are resilient. Today's kids have a multitude of problems—
everything from a broken home life to absentee parents. But
every morning most of them arrive at school wearing a smile.
They race through the halls, exchanging pleasantries with classmates. Adults arrive on the scene dressed in a frown. Instead of
good morning, they greet co-workers with a groan.

Divorce. Bills. Arguments. Pain. Sorrow. Traffic jams. Bad
jobs. You may not be able to control all circumstances, but you
can take command of your attitude.

Adults devote more time to complaining about their disad-
vantages than they do to counting their blessings. Life will never
be perfect. Make sure to navigate this world with hope. The way
to hope is through God.

One day when I was not in the best of moods, I happened
to turn on the computer. Up popped a photo of terminally ill
children. The first thing I noticed was their optimism. While
most of us are intolerant in times of trouble, these children
manage to smile through their woes.

When we moved to Pennsylvania, my parents had trouble
finding employment. Bills piled; rent was often deferred. Still, I
arose each morning, went out to play, and returned home with

the same optimistic mindset that most children have. I knew that the Lord would get us through. And He did. Every time.

Did you ever notice that when a child falls, they don't cry right away? Well, sometimes they do. But there are children who are not fazed—until they see an adult panic. That's when they lose it.

Adults make a habit out of being flustered. We are unnerved by the slightest dilemma. You get a flat tire. The coffee shop is out of your favorite brand. The cable is fuzzy. The Internet is slow. Your pants are too tight. We have a million excuses to lose hope. What if—stay with me here—we stopped complaining and just learned to live?

Once you allow something to rattle your nerves, what happens next? Usually, the day is ruined. And while you are attending a pity-party, time marches on.

Without being conscious of it, children live the way God intended—with a spirit full of anticipation. That is why they can dream without being affected by inconvenience. It is adults who convert innocent children to a darker path; adults who turn God's children away from His light.

Adults face barriers that test both endurance and patience. My fiction was criticized for being too commercial. Stories I submitted were rejected; some publishers did not bother to respond at all. At first, the realization of never achieving the status of professional writer sent me into the fetal position. Tears fell, tissues went into the wastepaper basket. Somewhere inside the child resurfaced. Suddenly, I recalled the carefree days when despite the glitches in my life, I wandered outside to a world full of expectation, a world where nothing could hold me back.

History is filled with dreamers who, like children, have never lost their exuberance. Nothing prevented them from walking on the moon, flying across the Atlantic, building the first airplane. Without an idealistic visualization, nothing can be accomplished.

When something does not go according to plan, don't let that alienate your inner peace. Be assured that God will light the way so that you will never be left in the dark.

If you fall, get back up. God does not promise that there will not be mountains to climb. He just asks that you remain vigilant.

"All your children shall be taught by the Lord, and
great shall be the peace of your children."
Isaiah 54

I'll Take Today

Cultivating a dream requires restraint. There is an inclination to rush through the process while daydreaming about distant possibilities. Doing so adds pressure to the journey. And if there is one thing you do not need it is more anxiety.

When I began my first novel in 2009, I envisioned its triumph and/or demise before the first paragraph was finished. I pondered the future, puzzling over how to find an agent, a publisher, what kind of query letter to write, whether anyone would like my book, and the likelihood of never being published at all.

Thinking too much can cause headaches. That is why the Lord asks that we take life as it comes. Losing sleep over what is beyond our control is a waste of time.

We are consumed by tomorrow while still getting through today. When anyone asks where I see myself in ten years, I remind them that because the future is not assured there is no way to answer that question. Agonizing over future happenings that may or may not take place will deplete your energy. Live in the moment. This moment.

In 2017, I was suffering from excruciating joint pain. My hands were useless; there were times when tying my own shoes seemed impossible. Terrified, I contacted my doctor to order bloodwork. One of the results indicated that I had lupus. There were additional blood tests to be done before lupus could be confirmed, but the idea of being ill shook me.

I didn't know how I would react if the diagnosis did not come back in my favor. How sick would I get? What if I couldn't finish school, or my book for that matter?

In the middle of my fret-fest, God reminded me that my life was in His hands, and I should be thankful for how far I had come: two college degrees along with a few published short stories.

Thankfully, I did not have lupus. The experience may have been God's way of teaching me not to skip ahead; to tread slowly through each moment, leaning on Him, not on myself. I almost failed the test, imagining all kinds of negative scenarios, giving up hope before a diagnosis could be concluded.

We begin each day with a mental list of tasks to accomplish, pondering what we need to do today, tomorrow, next year. . .

It is human nature to be apprehensive about a future not yet born, particularly in circumstances where you are behind in bills, lose your job, or endure any of the other demands thrown at you. Yet God tells us not to be anxious about anything. Being hassled over what is beyond your control will not solve the problem. But it will give you an ulcer or other health issues.

Technology, in a sense, has robbed us of the present moment, because it diverts our attention to a digital world complete with alarms and timers—reminders of what we must do in the days to come. We are in continual fast-forward mode. What about the current moment?

When you take the kids for a drive, rather than looking out the window, are their eyes are illuminated by a glowing screen? Nowadays cars have monitors so kids can watch their favorite

DVDs. Dad is consumed with the voice blaring from the GPS. Mom is texting. One thing they are not doing is talking to each other.

While at the doctor's office one afternoon, I noticed a family of five sitting across from me in the waiting room. Each family member held a phone that devoured their attention. My mind wandered to the days when my parents brought me to the doctor. Although there were no phones or fancy devices in those days, my parents could have written notes to communicate with me. They chose to use this instrument called a mouth, where the jaw moves at a rapid pace and sound emanates from the diaphragm. Guess what? I would answer them in complete sentences, too. What an amazing concept.

Lack of interaction will turn a family into strangers. I cherish the quality time I spent with my parents. On numerous occasions, I would sit at the kitchen table with my mother, sipping tea, and catching up on the day's events. My father and I took walks from one end of the city to the other. Pure quality time.

Today's kids would rather play video games than spend time with mom and dad. Some parents favor technology over real communication as well. But there are some things you cannot learn from a Smart Phone—like family history. Sure, you can research your genealogy online, but isn't it better to get it straight from the horse's mouth? Besides, archives will not contain personal stories.

Another time at a restaurant, I looked over at the table next to me. There sat a young couple in total silence, their heads bowed. I could tell right away they were not praying, and since their chests were heaving in and out, they were not dead either. No, they were staring down at their phones. Remember the days when couples held hands across the table, gazing into one another's eyes? Somehow the phone became a better partner.

With our minds churning in future events, our attention enveloped in the latest gadgets, there are few opportunities to be in the present moment. While you may be present physically, there is no emotional connection to the person you are with.

There is danger in not living in the moment—family and friends you are neglecting, places you are not seeing. You can look and not see the same way you can listen and not hear.

When is the last time you observed your surroundings? My favorite way to unwind is to get out of the man-made world and retreat into the natural one. Hiking is a great means of rejuvenation. There is something therapeutic about being immersed in nature where a soft breeze drowns out the clamor of society.

Animals recognize the beauty of the natural world more than humans. Not that I can pretend to know how they feel, but I guarantee they are not worried about the future. They live in the moment while enjoying the splendor of their environment.

Trees, flowers, sunsets, rainbows—these beautiful wonders are lost on us because we see past them. It would serve us well to learn from God's other creatures. They take time to imbibe the Lord's precious gifts without concern of what lies ahead. They are right where they need to be. In the moment.

Death is another distraction. On one hand, reflecting on one's mortality is not a bad thing. Understanding that tomorrow is not promised will make you appreciate the present even more. But some of us waste so much time sweating death that we forget to live. Yes, all of us have to die, whether we like it or not. Be cautious not to devote too much time speculating on when the Grim Reaper will strike, because your life will pass you by. As my grandmother used to say, "Time waits for no one."

Some people are so consumed by their impending fate that they spend countless hours trying to avoid death. They refuse to fly, take a cruise, or do anything that might, in their view, bring them closer to death's door. By harboring angst about the inevitability of death, they have put life on hold.

Imagine if Jesus had allowed fear to overcome Him? If He felt any trepidation, He did not succumb to it. He seized the moment to carry out His Father's plans. There were lepers to cleanse, demons to cast out, illnesses to cure, sermons to teach, enemies to forgive. Jesus could not have performed His tasks by panicking. He understood that each moment gone is one that cannot be regained.

Being preoccupied with the future is not the only waste of time; there is another thief known as regret. While worry keeps you concentrated on what is ahead, regret keeps you bound to what has passed. Healthy regret signals a conscience. It lets you analyze your behavior so that you can make amends. God's most endearing quality is His ability to forgive. He does not want you to be defined by sin.

Unhealthy regret confines you to a lifetime of purgatory. You're transported to the past where every sin you committed is relived again and again. Living in the past is like being on a treadmill. You may feel like you're moving, but in reality, you are getting nowhere.

The way to move forward is to treat mistakes like a traffic light. Yellow is God telling you to slow down long enough to acknowledge your transgressions. Red is God telling you to stop and ask His forgiveness. Green is God's sign that you are free to move on.

Just as Jesus was not consumed by the future, He did not misuse time by living for yesterday. Though there were plenty of reasons for Jesus to glance back—the loss of his earthly father Joseph for example—He knew that the past was dead. Why live for something that isn't there? We can learn from Jesus by giving thanks for the present moment; by honoring God in how we operate in the time He has given us.

Make peace with yesterday by living for today, accepting that the future is uncertain. Healthy planning can be done without going too far. So, make your lists. Just take it one step, or one moment, at a time. Be sure to take notice of life's ambiance—watch a sunrise or sunset, listen to the rain, gaze at the mountains in the distance, or the stars up above. Most of all, do not permit the past to devour you, do not permit the future to overwhelm you. One is gone, the other not promised.

"You have no idea what your life will be like tomorrow. You are a puff of smoke that appears briefly and then disappears."
James 4:14

Think, Become

Thoughts can be a generous ally or a vindictive enemy. Pessimism can cause irreparable damage. A negative person's words can shatter our confidence. That is nothing compared to what we tell ourselves.

For years I questioned my potential. When I graduated high school, I convinced myself that I was not smart enough to succeed in college. Even writing took a backseat for a brief time after I allowed myself to think that someone like me could never become a writer. Because of my diffidence, I spent countless hours wallowing in self-doubt when I should have had confidence in my capabilities.

The same thing happened whenever I went out for a new job, including teaching. I thought, "No one will ever hire me." In my opinion, the other applicants had more talent, brains, and a better personality. Except I did get hired, and when I started teaching, some teachers put me on their list as one of the first subs to call.

There were plenty of occasions when I could have made lasting friendships. Unfortunately, I was reluctant to engage in social events. It was common for me to come up with excuses as to why I could not attend gatherings such as dinners. Eating in front of people was awkward. What if I dribbled or spit food at someone? And when I did make an appearance, my conversation was terse, as I never felt I had anything interesting to say.

My days of wanting to be an actress came up short on two occasions. By second grade, I begged my mother to take me to the city to try out for commercials. She didn't want me acting professionally until I was old enough. That didn't stop her from encouraging me to try out for my school's production of *The Wizard of Oz*.

To my surprise, I got a part and managed to make it through two rehearsals. Running all over the stage caused embarrassment. The other kids seemed so much more brilliant in their roles. This is what I told myself. I left the play soon after. It made me wonder how I would ever audition for real projects if I couldn't even play the part of a flying monkey in a school play.

Years later, there was a place called *The Actor's Lab* that charged $10 per acting lesson. It was down the street from my job. I quit after one lesson, telling myself that I didn't have the extra money. The truth was I got nervous when I had to deliver a monologue.

How you view yourself affects how others see you. A reserved demeanor might give the impression that you have no interest in socialization. Showing your boss that you're afraid to take on added responsibilities will not get you the promotion you've been waiting for.

My parents were two of the greatest influences in my life. But what they gave to me they could not give to themselves. Mom and Dad lacked self-assurance. My father was committed to the notion that he was not intelligent just as my mother believed she was not pretty.

Some years ago, I found two journals that belonged to my parents. Sometime before I was born, they had gone on a couple's retreat with the local church. They were encouraged to write their feelings in a journal. I hesitated before reading the entries because they were my parents' private thoughts. What I discovered filled me with sadness.

My mother wrote about her envy of other women. She was despondent over her looks, her weight, how she dressed, and her inability to carry children. One of my mother's dreams was to have a family. She worried constantly that it would never happen. The first few years of marriage were difficult because her pregnancies ended in miscarriage.

Much like my mother, Dad's outlook did not differ. He described himself as feeling "lower than everyone else." He feared that people would laugh at him for not being smart. After we moved to Pennsylvania, my father took a civil service exam for a new job. He told himself that he would fail. And he did.

As I said in a previous chapter, I am not ashamed of my parents because of the things they did not have. But my heart is heavy knowing that they went through life feeling inept. What they thought of themselves carried consequences, perhaps even leading to missed opportunities.

Rejection can be harsh in a society that worships victory. At one time, I vowed never to write again if my work went unnoticed. That attitude produced distrust in my creative abilities. So what if I am never published again? So what if my work is read by a few people, not a multitude? That will not stop me from doing what I love most. Not anymore.

There are times when the procession is more important than the succession. You don't have to be a winner to enjoy the game. Everything we do adds to the journey. If you don't become a professional basketball player, God is not saying that you shouldn't play basketball anymore. You can't succeed without trying first, and you will never try anything if you don't believe in yourself.

We can imagine Mary Magdalene's hesitance in following Jesus. According to some, she was far from a model citizen. Whether this is true is up for debate. For the sake of argument, let's suppose it is true. Mary's thoughts might have deceived her into thinking that Jesus would not find her acceptable. To Mary's surprise, Jesus showed her respect. She became one of His most trusted disciples, and it was Mary to whom Jesus appeared after His resurrection.

Fill your mind with encouraging thoughts. Tell yourself that you are good enough, strong enough, and capable enough. Should your dreams fall short of your expectations, know that God has His reasons, which do not include you being a failure.

"Blessed is the man who trusts in the Lord, whose hope is the Lord."
Jeremiah 17:7

Humility Goes a Long Way

It can be gratifying watching your goals come to fruition. The first time my prose reached print I was elated. Things really started to take off when my first novel was published. Suddenly my name was all over Google, and people I had not heard from in years touched base to congratulate me. As I settled into the role of *published author*, I was quick not to allow the adulation to obliterate my humility.

While there is nothing wrong with celebrating your achievements, modesty, as they say, is the best policy. An occasional pat on the back can boost your confidence. But seeking constant applause is a disservice to God. Dreams are an extension of God's purpose for our lives. Be careful not to misuse them for your "own" glory.

Success can be a double-edged sword. It can take you places you've never been, or it can bite you in places you've never imagined. Too much power can inflate the ego. It is up to the dreamer to seek eternal understanding on how to handle unexpected recognition.

There are plenty of people who wouldn't know humility if it came up and introduced itself. A high-ranking position, for example, does not place you above someone with a lesser status. After all, what's in a title? You may have more skills, make better money, but we put our pants on one leg at a time.

We all know at least one person who walks around with a swelled head. The nose goes up, the humility comes down. Being a published author does not make me better than those struggling to find a home for their words, because I know there are far better writers than me.

My parents' struggles kept them humble. Even when they were working, they never criticized anyone for not having a job because they understood what it was like to be judged unfairly. My mother would give you her last dollar without questioning why you had no money. In fact, Mom was probably the least materialistic person I had ever known. She never went to a store looking for designer clothes. Never bought extravagant objects for the house. Any money she spent usually was on someone else's behalf.

One day I got on social media and discovered a photo of a woman sitting in the park. Someone had taken the picture without her permission. The caption for the photo read: "Your tax dollars at work." Insert eye roll here—that's what I did when I saw this particular post. Maybe the woman lost her job. Maybe she was on a lunch break. Maybe she had a terminal illness and just wanted a place to think.

Our rush to judge others without knowing the full story has come full-circle with the birth of social media. My parents' hard times taught me an important lesson: Not everyone sitting in the park on a sunny afternoon is milking the government. Yes, there are unfortunate incidences where people take advantage of the system. But it is not for us to judge. And it's not going to affect me one way or the other.

Growing up, my family had a lot of conversations around the dining room table. I can assure you that none of the dialogue consisted of who paid taxes and who did not. Perhaps people had more important things to discuss in those days. Perhaps social media has saturated us with content that seeps into our minds until we cannot think about anything else.

The Lord giveth and the Lord taketh away. None of us are exempt from losing a vocation. Just because you have a good job today doesn't mean you will hold on to it. You hear about it all the time, an unforeseen illness, a tragic event. POOF—the career is no more. The house you take pride in can go into foreclosure; the car can be repossessed. Unemployment lines do not discriminate, so never get so high up the ladder that you can't see your way back down again.

Dreams can be taken away in an instant. The more success you have the more humble you should be. If you are lucky enough to share your gifts with the rest of humanity, then you owe a debt of gratitude to the Lord.

No one had more talent than Jesus. If walking on water doesn't put you above others, I don't know what does. His importance as the son of God did not outweigh His humility. And He asks the same of us.

Whether you sing, cure, write, or own a company—humility goes a long way. Don't flaunt, share. Don't brag, give thanks. Remembering where you come from and where you are headed will keep you humble.

"When pride comes, disgrace comes, but
with the humble is wisdom."
Proverbs 11:2

Being Grateful

I am thankful for . . . You can fill in the blanks with your own list. My hope is that you fill a few pages.

People gripe more than they express joy. No one likes a sour puss, but we all wear one from time to time. I talked a little about this in the chapter "The Child Within." Being grateful for God's blessings is imperative if you want to stay humble. Give thanks for food, shelter, clothing, air, dreams—everything.

Did you ever know anyone with so much money they couldn't possibly spend it all in one lifetime? Their spending habits involve luxurious cars, enormous homes, lavish boats—anything that would make the average person blush. Yet they never seem grateful.

My first apartment was a four-room box that had mold growing on the base of the walls. I couldn't afford to fill the rooms with elaborate décor. Whatever modest belongings I had were hand-me-downs or purchased from a dollar store.

One Christmas I paid twenty dollars for a sorry excuse of a tree because it was all I could afford. Think Charlie Brown (OK, so mine was a little bigger), but still pathetic. The point is, once the tree was trimmed, once the decorations were in place, my apartment was a sight to behold. I would sit on the couch, sipping hot cocoa, carols blasting from the radio, grateful for the beautiful sights and sounds of Christmas.

My father did not have much money. His apartment also contained items that would never be found on Park Avenue. Yet he was proud of the little he had. A far cry from those who are well-off but appreciate nothing.

I knew of such people. They had enough and too much. They had something else, too—attitude. Somehow having millions of dollars did not bring them to their knees with gratitude. The used their wealth to show off. No smiles, no graciousness, no meekness. If you think money can buy you personality, you should have met these people. Talk about wet mops!

When is the last time you gave thanks for the little things? One afternoon while I was sipping tea in my favorite café, I made a list of things that brought me bliss. On my list was English Breakfast Tea, since a good cup of a warm beverage makes me smile. Other things included music, books, writing, going for walks, playing tennis, looking at the stars, birds chirping in the morning, crickets chirping at night.

It occurred to me that we don't give thanks for simple things like the joy a song brings or the feeling we get when walking in nature. And when is the last time you noticed anyone expressing gratitude for being given a dream, especially a dream that never comes to pass?

We are on this earth for a nanosecond. There is no time to be ungrateful. God has given more blessings than we are willing to admit. That alone is enough to give praise. Should I never write again, I am beholden to the time spent with pen in hand. My journey as a writer may not last, but what a ride it has been!

Saying goodbye to someone you love after they pass away is painful. There comes a time when you should give thanks for having known that person at all. My mother was with me for twelve years, which doesn't sound like a lot of time. I had moments when I felt cheated for not having her around longer.

Then I thought about the kids who never had a mother at all. No memories of being rocked. No birthday parties. No holidays. Let's not forget the kids who are trapped in abysmal circumstances: abuse, neglect, etc. The quantity of years I spent with my mother wasn't as important as the quality. We did more in twelve years than most parents do with their children in fifty.

When my mother died, my maternal grandmother stepped in to help raise me. At the end of every school year, she would send for me, and I'd spend the entire summer at her house in Florida. While most of my peers were hanging around the neighborhood, I was grateful to be sitting on the patio with my second mother, talking about old memories.

My great-aunts lived around the corner, and I would wander over to their house where we would listen to big band music on the record player, watch old movies, and talk. A favorite topic was my love of writing. My aunts always gave me a pep talk to cheer on my dreams.

God expects you to be grateful for friends and family, jobs and homes. And your dreams, too, whether they come true or not. The incentive is not the actual completion of a dream, but the thrill of loving something so much, you do it no matter what.

"Every perfect gift is from above, coming
down from the Father of lights."
Ephesians 5:30

Ambition

Ambition can be a positive characteristic, until you turn it into an unhealthy one. It will compel you to accomplish the impossible. When your dreams cause you to overlook more important priorities like family, friends, and morals—ambition develops into a vice.

The main objective in any sport is to beat the opposing team. Winning is everything. Just like actors who nervously await to see if they will take home the Academy Award. Loss does not bring out the best in people. Some react in anger by lashing out at their competitors. Nothing screams sore loser more than a bad attitude.

I am not going to pretend that winning isn't exciting. But if all your effort amounts to is being number one, then you are too ambitious.

I never had to worry about bringing home my grades. My father could tell when I had tried my hardest. If he saw me slacking, he would advise me to study harder. When he knew that I had done my best, he was satisfied. A seventy average in math never got me into trouble. Just the opposite. Dad would praise me because he knew math was not my best subject.

My parents never compared me to other kids, either. They never pressured me to be the best so they could brag to their comrades. All they required of me was an honest attempt.

The summer my mother died, I played on a softball team. My father came to every game, despite his aversion to sports. One time I was having an off day, striking out every time I stepped up to bat. After three innings, the coach made the mistake of letting me pitch. I threw grapefruits the entire inning. After the game, I met up with my father. He said, "You did well." Dad didn't care whether I was a winner; all that mattered was my love of softball.

His attitude was the total antithesis of a fellow teammate's father. She enjoyed the game, at first. Then her father made her practice throwing the ball for hours, rain or shine. Whenever her game was not up to par, he would condemn her, until playing softball lost its allure.

Ambition can lead to envy. Being too ambitious about your career, for instance, will possess your motivation until you no longer care who you step on to get what you want. It is like pouring too much salt on your food. It may taste good in the beginning, but the more salt you add, the more bitter your food becomes.

Envy does not come without consequence. When you sever relationships, or worse, break the law, you have failed God's plan. The willingness to fight for a dream does not include putting up decency as collateral.

Knocking someone for having a dream is also considered envious. I have endured my share of remarks when it came to being a writer. Initially, I was angry at some of the things that were said to me. It took time to realize that the insults were manifested out of jealousy.

Dreams are God's contribution. He expects you to work hard to meet His objectives without the risk of losing your soul, er without the rivalry ambition can lead to. Ambition needs to be tempered by faith. In your pursuit of a dream, stay true to yourself. And to God.

*"Where jealousy and selfish ambition exist, there
is disorder and every foul practice."*
James 3:16

Seek and You Shall Find

Some people play a major role in our lives while others play a bit part. God brings each person to teach a lesson—both good and bad. If a naysayer's function is to condemn a dream, a mentor will increase a mentee's motivation.

Youngsters often look up to celebrities as heroes, adorning their bedrooms with posters of their favorite actors and actresses. They mimic a celebrity's behavior, appearance, and lexicon.

Picture me at six, grabbing my father's tape recorder, taking one of my toy guitars, and singing 9 to 5 at the top of my lungs. Dolly Parton was one of my early heroes. My father's treasured possession was his record player. He frequently played his albums in the living room for me and my mother. I can still see Dad sitting in his chair, silently mouthing lyrics, and Mom lying on the couch, bobbing her head to the music. And then there was me with a turkey baster as a microphone, pretending to be Dolly.

My mother was influenced by her favorite movie idols, whom she tried to imitate. When she was fourteen, she took her eight-year-old brother to see *The Music Man*. The movie left my mother awestruck, and as they left the theater, she went into a marching stance and started belting out "Seventy-Six Trombones," much to her brother's chagrin.

We can all recall a time as kids when we yearned to be someone other than ourselves.

However, being influenced is not reserved merely for the young at heart. Adults are also impressionable. The next time you buy a product in a store, think about where you first heard about or saw that item: book, television, magazine, radio, the Internet?

Should you require further proof that adults are impressionable, check out social media. You will stumble upon posts that express both positive and negative messages. Think in terms of memes. One person decides to create a photo with a catchphrase. Once it is posted, another person sees it, then shares it on their page, then the next, until it goes viral. Some memes encourage love. Some inspire hate. On any given day you will find offensive subject matter, disparaging anyone with differing qualities or living conditions.

Mentors serve as guides professionally, socially, and emotionally. The trick is to recognize the good from the not so good. Not everybody who crosses your path will take you in the right direction. Some will promise great riches in exchange for your soul.

We imbibe much of what we see and hear. It is our job to monitor whom we emulate. Be cautious when choosing a mentor. It should be someone you respect who will respect you in return.

Mentors can be people in our personal lives as well. I was blessed with parents who believed in me. When I announced at five that I wanted to be a singer like Dolly Parton, my mother could have said, "Yeah, I have a bridge I want to sell you." On her deathbed she told me to become that singer. When my dream shifted to acting, my father said, "Go for it" not "Get real!" My Great-Aunt Anna did not tell me to put down the pen because I could not string together a sentence worth a penny.

She urged me to pursue writing. My grandmother never hesitated to remind me that I was as good as anyone else.

Teachers are some of the more common mentors we have. In kindergarten, my regular teacher fell down the stairs and broke her leg. Since she couldn't finish out the year, a male sub took her place. I can't exactly tell you why I was mesmerized by this guy, but I looked up to him—and not just because I was short.

With my mother on the PTA, she made friends with the faculty at school. Before I knew it, she invited my kindergarten sub over to our house for dinner. In those days, I was a complete introvert, afraid to speak to anyone. Yes, I admired the guy, but that didn't mean I was ready to break bread with him.

Inside my bedroom I could hear my parents conversing with my teacher. I wanted to come out and speak to him. What exactly do you say to a teacher when they're impersonating a civilian? Finally, an idea popped into my head. I got my portable record player, plugged it in, and pushed it into the kitchen while I remained hidden behind the wall in the living room.

The conversation stopped. I stretched out my tiny hand to put the needle on the record. The music started. With a peering eye, I saw my mother bring her hand up to her mouth to cover a giggle. My father sipped coffee and shook his leg underneath the table. For some reason, my way of communicating with my teacher was through the song "Ebony and Ivory."

Mentors do that. They make you reach for the impossible dream, or play songs that convey brotherhood.

In high school, one of my English teachers greatly influenced my reading list. Already an avid reader, this teacher familiarized me with the likes of Shakespeare, Dickens, Hugo, and Christie, among others. Before the class would read a great work of literature, we would study the writer's life. All these years later, I am still reading biographies on some of the greatest minds in literary history. Because this teacher was a mentor, I ended up being an English major in college. It is amazing the effect someone can have on you.

My greatest mentor is God. When I fall, He picks me up. When I doubt, He brings me hope. When I take a wrong turn, He sets me on the right path. Since dreams come from God, they must be applied in a way that is pleasing to Him.

A good mentor is inclined to share their faith. If you see someone in desperate need of rescue, share the good news that God loves them. Passing on messages of love can have an ever-lasting impact—one much healthier than posting distressing memes.

Jesus teaches us to be patient, forgiving, loving, accepting. He tells us not to judge, hate, or take revenge. We are all created equal in the eyes of the Lord. As a Christian mentor, you should never use faith as a weapon. The Jesus portrayed in the Bible is not always the one some Christians choose to follow. Instead, they manipulate the gospel to mirror their own views. Violence, anger, and bigotry are not characteristics of Christianity. Being a *Christian* mentor means imitating Jesus. Words and actions matter. Heal don't hurt. Love don't hate.

I mentioned that there is a difference between advice and control. Naysayers control, which is why they criticize. Mentors advise you in ways that will increase your self-confidence. When I was in college, several of my professors knew about my writing aspirations. They instructed me on how to establish connections so that I could take the next step in my career. Without their mentorship I would not have known how to get published.

Although mentors can be positive role models, they are human beings capable of mistakes. We hold people in such high regard that when they fail to meet our expectations, we become unnerved. Think about a time when your favorite athlete let you down. Or an actor who did not quite live up to the image depicted in your mind. You might stop watching sports or attending movies. Some people stop listening to a singer's music if that person does not endorse a specific political candidate.

Our habitual need to worship another person can be misleading. On the surface they appear flawless: perfect body, hair, skin tone—thriving and self-assured. We are in awe of their superhuman abilities. They can do no wrong—until, of course, they do. Disappointment sets in. Their failings become ours as well.

When you begin worshipping another human being, you create a false god in your mind. Looking up to a notable figure is fine, but if you feel compelled to knock someone's block off because they don't share your interest, then there's a problem. You are not related to the person you are fighting over. They don't even know you exist.

People will let you down. Though it is wise to choose a mentor with ethical behavior, they will never be a saint. Even saints were not saints at first.

"Walk with wise men and you will become wise, but
the companion of fools suffers harm."
Proverbs 13:20

The Age of a Dream

"The only time life stops is when you die." That line from my novel *Look Back to Yesterday* may have been written for a character, but its message denotes the spirit of a dreamer. When I went for my M.A. at forty, age was not a deterrent. I had discovered as an undergraduate that the number of years one has lived does not determine their ability to acquire skills. Nor does it limit the potential of a dream.

Have you or someone you know been tempted to do something but used age as an excuse not to? Don't misunderstand, as we get older our bodies weaken, our strength declines. Maybe you can't lift two-hundred-pound weights anymore, but you can still attend college when you're eighty.

Responsibilities can stall a dream. I had the opportunity to get a higher education after high school. Thanks to fear, I chickened out. Once my father's health grew worse, I was too busy taking care of his needs to make time for college. Fortunately, God awarded me more time to pursue my dreams.

You may have put off your dreams as well. The important thing is that you pick up where you left off. Whether you are fifty, sixty, or ninety—take your dreams off the backburner. You want to be a student? Be one. If you can't afford college, borrow books from your local library. Schooling doesn't necessarily have to take place inside a classroom.

Do you wish to travel? Go for it—if money permits. If not, do not hesitate to get books on other states or countries. Watching documentaries is another good idea. Never allow age to slow you down. Become a preacher, a teacher, take a hike, ride a bike, go deep sea fishing, sail around the world.

Should you encounter a naysayer reminding you of your age, tell them not to pick out the casket anytime soon.

When my aunt decided to move from Brooklyn to Florida in her mid-sixties, she had some reservations about relocating. Her dream was to buy her first home in a warm climate. It could not have been easy moving to a new venue after living in Brooklyn for more than sixty years.

While on the plane, she sat next to a couple around her age. They struck up a conversation and ended up friends by the time the flight landed. As luck would have it, the couple was moving to the same community as my aunt. They shared a wonderful friendship for the duration of their lives.

Had age limited my aunt's dream, she wouldn't have moved to Florida where she went on to meet many close confidants. She was not ashamed that she had to wait until retirement before she could afford her first home, either. Better late than never.

A friend of my grandmother's dreamed of traveling without public transportation. She studied for her driver's test and at sixty-five became a driver. Her first car was a small, used vehicle. She used to call my grandmother her "co-pilot" as they buckled up and took off through Florida's streets. Many times she visited friends in other cities, delighting in her new-found independence.

I worked for two attorneys in their mid-eighties. The office showed no signs of modernity. There were no computers, fax machines, nothing of modern convenience. I had to type wills and deeds on an old typewriter. Sometimes I overheard people questioning why these two old men were still practicing law when they could be enjoying the fruits of their labor. Both had done really well and money was not a concern.

As young men, they had a dream to become lawyers. In old age, the dream was still alive. It didn't matter that they used canes to walk, had hearing loss, and couldn't see without thick coke bottles for glasses. Of course, my grandmother had her own opinion on why they were still working—men are pests and wives don't want them around the house. But that's another story!

Age is not justification for putting off your dreams. When I prayed for enlightenment after losing my father, God did not say, "You're too old to go back to school." He told me to get to it.

All a dream requires is inner strength. Have faith that God knows what He is doing.

"Although our outer self is wasting away, yet our
inner self is being renewed day by day."
2 Corinthians 4:16-17

Committing to a Dream

Much of what we do in life requires commitment. You sign a lease when you rent an apartment, agreeing to live there a certain length of time. When you get married, you make a vow to honor your spouse. Having children entails caring for them until they are of legal age to fend for themselves.

Dreams, too, involve commitment.

In the beginning, my writing schedule lacked promise. There was always an excuse to put off my work: laundry, too much noise, TV. The absence of any real commitment left empty pages.

Graduate school changed all that. My work had to be turned in on specific days. It was quite a task trying to finish ten, twenty-page papers on time, but I got the job done. One of the takeaways from the program was that I learned to write every single day. Today, I have a writing planner where I keep track of how much I write each week.

Commitments are made from the beginning of our lives to the end. Children are implored to clean their rooms; adolescents to keep curfews. The house you live in was built by someone committed to building it. You commit to making a trip to the grocery store to stock up on supplies.

Do you lack discipline? Give yourself a deadline, much like when you have a project due at work. You either fulfill your obligation or risk getting fired.

Here's an exercise to try: Get out a piece of paper—or, like me, a journal—write 2-3 goals for the day. Think of God as your boss (which He is!). Write something along the lines of "Dear God, today I am going to clean out the basement, or today I am going to run three miles." Should you not meet a goal, give yourself a repercussion. No ice-cream for dessert. No television after dinner. Better yet—no phone (there's a frightening punishment!). Does that sound juvenile? Probably. Whatever it takes to get yourself in the groove.

My desire to sing as a child drove me to perform constantly. I was committed to a dream, albeit not the right one, but I digress. I'd run into the bathroom (good acoustics) with my mother's turkey baster, point the round bulb toward my mouth, and sing my heart out. There was so much excitement in my performance, I paid little attention to anything else, like dropping the baster in the toilet. Don't worry, I dried it off and put it back in the kitchen drawer. When Thanksgiving rolled around, my poor mother had no idea what she was squirting on the turkey.

Acting was another dream I dedicated myself to. I watched television shows and would act them out in my bedroom, reciting lines so loud that when my father had company, people would ask him who I was talking to upstairs. I read books on acting, wrote plays, screenplays (technically, I wrote the sequel to *Back to the Future* when I was eleven. The proof is sitting in one of my old Garbage Pail Kids folders somewhere).

The Lord is committed to you, hence the reason He has given you a dream. He knows you can get the job done. Show

Him that you are devoted to your dreams by employing a good work ethic, and trust that He will do His part.

When you want something, commit to it. Without serious commitment, your dreams will fail. Dreams deserve one hundred percent. So does God.

How can you play a guitar well without practice? How will you pass a test without studying? What good is dreaming without obligation? I can sit around all day thinking about the book I need to write. Thinking is not committing. Doing is committing.

Make a pledge right now to do what you can for God's gift. Just remember, finalizing your dreams is up to you. The Lord can give you a nudge, but He cannot make you do anything without your commitment.

"Entrust your works to the Lord, and your plans will succeed."
Proverbs 16:3

The Calm Before the Storm

When I started writing this book in the summer of 2019, promising things were on the horizon. I was feeling refreshed having just come back from a much-needed beach vacation. A funny thing happens at the ocean: the chaos of the world melts in the sun, and the residue gets washed away by giant waves. There is nothing like a vast ocean to remind us how miniscule we are.

I began subbing again in the fall three days per week. The other two days were left open for revisions on my novel, which was slated for release in May 2020. In the meantime, I had various activities to keep me occupied, but first I had to overcome double pinkeye and a stomach bug that kept my head in a bucket for over twenty-four hours.

In November, I gave a reading from my manuscript at a Writers' Showcase and left early to attend a Judy Collins concert. Three weeks later I was in the audience at a Trisha Yearwood concert. A few weeks after that, Mannheim Steamroller came to town. Being a Christmas fanatic, I bought tickets to that, too.

There was also a trip to New York City where Christmas truly comes alive. I walked to 34th Street, gazing in the windows of Macy's. Next, Rockefeller Center followed by the tree lighting in Bryant Park. There was music, lights, hot chocolate, and a multitude of little shops. Regardless of the chill in the air, I was besieged by a beautiful introduction to the upcoming holiday.

New Year's Eve has never been a favorite of mine. I am usually sound asleep by nine o'clock. I managed to stay awake by stuffing myself with snacks like pepperoni, provolone, and an Oreo McFlurry.

Though I had never put much stock into ushering in the New Year—since every day is a new beginning anyway—2020 sounded like a good number, a year full of possibilities. I wanted to welcome it, embrace it, thank the hidden months that would turn me into an author at last.

It went against what I believed, forecasting an unknown future, yet the year seemed assuring—at least in my mind.

February 2020: Plans were underway for my upcoming book. There would be a book launch along with a party. I made a list of people to invite, scoped out venues for the celebration, inquired about caterers, found a bakery that made cakes in the shape of books. It was all coming together the way I had envisioned.

Early March 2020: Edits on my manuscript were afoot. In need of more time, I cut back on subbing to two days a week. Sleeping was slashed to five hours per night. By 5 A.M., I was at Dunkin Donuts securing a large tea, hoping the caffeine would wake me from my fog. By 7 A.M., I was at the computer; my fingers sailed across the keyboard, pounding away at new scenes while deleting old ones.

The taxing schedule bequeathed dark circles underneath my eyes and inhabited most of my attention. No wonder I hadn't heard of this new thing called coronavirus. Even after awareness kicked in, I paid it no mind. It was a virus like any other virus. You sneezed, coughed, blew your nose and got on with things.

Teachers started falling ill from the stomach bug and pinkeye, the same illnesses that had plagued me weeks earlier. There were plenty of sub jobs to go around, but I was still committed to my manuscript.

Friday, March 13, 2020: It was a day like any other, save for the full moon and the bad omen attached to the number 13. I was subbing for elementary art when the principal announced that all classes would conclude for at least a week. Then it was over to the copying machine to make packets for the students to take home so they could keep up with their studies.

I left work thinking that a week's vacation would be ideal, giving me extra time to put final edits on my manuscript. When I stopped at the mall to order a large pizza, chairs were being placed on top of tables, floors swept, last minute meals prepared.

What was the fuss about?

That night I sat down to watch the news, grasping for the first time that the virus was no joke. The world was on lockdown. Movie theaters, churches, and libraries closed their doors. Grocery stores stayed open. Shoppers scrambled to secure loaves of bread and rolls of toilet paper. I hadn't seen so much rushing around since Cabbage Patch Kids hit stores in the eighties.

Outside I noticed minor changes like streets devoid of people, cars—anything that could move. The Internet was abuzz with photos of other states administering the same routine.

With Times Square as a ghost town, the severity of the virus hit home. Broadway marquees went dark. Familiar restaurants stopped producing popular delicacies. Throngs of people disappeared inside their homes.

Like everyone else, I wondered how long the lockdown would sustain—three weeks tops, I thought. Then March turned into April, April into May, spring into summer.

No one saw the train coming, the one that brought the world to its knees. We were all thrown back in our seats, leveled by a new unexplained virus. How could this happen? Maybe in pervious centuries, but not now. We were indestructible, undefeated. We had come so far in modern science. Yet we were reduced to helplessness as the disease claimed so many lives.

There were new norms like masks and social distancing. Along with these concessions came anger, accusations, anxiety, and discontent. Everyone shouting but no one listening. So much disinformation and misinformation being thrown at us, it was hard to discern fact from fiction.

Every now and then something beyond our comprehension comes along to remind us that the Father is at the helm. We can do nothing except through Him. The future is not something we can predict nor control.

In the face of a crisis, we rely on our own maniacal need to micromanage. But we are nothing more than flesh, blood, and bone. Our lives are in God's hands. Once we accept this, we can make the best of the conditions we find ourselves in.

"In his hand is the soul of every living thing, and
the life breath of all mankind?"
Job 12:10

Changing Course

The fantasy: My novel is published and receives rave reviews. After the book launch, a party, where family and friends gush over my magnum opus. My guests enjoy a feast of chicken sautéed in butter and garlic sauce, baby carrots, and three types of salads. A large, rectangular cake is wheeled out with a photo of my book resting on top. I take to the podium to read a selection from my novel. Everyone is at full attention, staring up at me— the shy girl from Brooklyn who finally made good. In the middle of my reading in walks Dolly Parton, my favorite country singer. She'd heard that I am a huge fan, so she arranged a special trip to meet me. We take photos together, she signs autographs, then offers her best wishes before getting back on her bus.

The reality: Coronavirus prevented any type of book promotion. No readings, no lectures, no party with Dolly Parton crashing it. No guidelines on how to promote a book in a lockdown. All forms of personal appearances stalled. The new narrative contained a plot twist but proposed no ending.

Until the pandemic, I had planned on doing readings in New York City. With no shortage of bookstores or cafes, New York is a mecca for writers. I had done a reading there in 2018. At the time, I stayed at the Paramount Hotel in Times Square. After a ten-minute recitation from my essay "The Dream Lives

On," I hopped a subway headed for the hotel. The next morning, I awoke in time to catch the sunrise. It was the end of summer; the hot sun beat upon my faintly tanned arms. At a nearby deli, I grabbed a quick breakfast of oatmeal, eggs, and orange juice, then took my feast to Bryant Park where I ate secluded behind a copy of *The New York Times*.

By the time my novel was published, New York had closed its doors, much like the rest of the country. People everywhere pounded their fists at the air. At first, I was among the angry flock, wishing that instead of being sheltered at home, I could travel the states with my new book.

Then, a sense of calm swept over me. It was a new emotion; one I had not practiced in the past. Although I was saddened about having to cancel literary festivities, the show was far from over. I had to come up with a new plan.

Copies of my book arrived ready to sign. Seated at the dining room table, I autographed forty-five paperbacks. Despite not being inside a bookstore, I made the best of it. The party was back on, too; a small gathering in my backyard with trays of pizza, and thanks be to God, I got a cake bearing the cover of my book.

News of my book began to spread. Then came promotional opportunities like virtual readings for local libraries, along with a radio interview over the phone. Not conventional self-promotion, but it worked.

While in quarantine, I continued writing this book. Though I admit to occasional bouts of doubt, wondering if it made sense to waste time writing, I prayed until God took me by the hand and sat me at the computer.

Yeah, the news looked bad—death, destruction, hate. Every day while I waited for the world to end, it kept turning. I heard the words of my Great-Aunt Anna echoing through my mind: "This too shall pass."

Like many of you, my mind sailed backward and forward. The past looked inviting, the future chilling. We wanted to go back to happier days or skip to the end of the virus. We could do neither. God said to be still.

Sacrifice is part of being a child of God. If Jesus could bear nails through His hands and feet, a crown of thorns upon His head, we could wear masks; we could stay indoors to keep an illness from spreading; we could adjust dreams.

Maybe you had dreams that ended up on the shelf because of coronavirus or another unforeseen emergency. God will never forsake you. Modifying a dream does not suggest the end of a dream. Let faith act as a bridge so that you can safely cross to the other side.

"Those whose steps are guided by the Lord may stumble, but they will never fall, for the Lord holds their hand."
Psalm 37:23-24

God's Greatest Lessons

The pandemic invited much needed introspection. There was a wealth of time to deliberate on what I had learned since taking my first steps onto a college campus armed with a dream.

Time is of the essence. My mother's death at thirty-nine and my father's deteriorating health made me aware of my mortality. There is no timeframe on how long we will walk the earth. Putting off a dream may result in no dream at all.

Here are the top three lessons God taught me:

Endurance: The loss of my father was not meant to cripple me. Though his journey ended, mine had just begun. God turned my weaknesses into strengths, my darkest moments into my most defining moments.

Patience: Whenever I became anxious, wanting to speed through time and see where I would end up, God said, *"Be still."* Life works best when it goes in accordance with His clock.

Reliance: Along came the naysayers to crush my dreams. The Lord urged me to ignore negative voices and rely on Him instead.

Summary

- **Life Goes On:** No matter what you are going through, God will strengthen you through faith. Keep your chin up and solider on.

- **God's Blueprint:** There is a plan for your life. God's incessant messages will come by way of thoughts, dreams, or other people. If you notice a pattern of communication coming your way, it is likely that God is vying for your attention. Stop and listen.

- **Watch For Cynics:** Know the difference between those who pull you out of the water and those who push you under. Advice informs, not disparages. Don't allow another person's insecurities to break you.

- **Be Not Afraid:** Fear is a restraint, a vice that shrinks your dreams. Overcome rather than succumb. Use fear as fuel. Give your dreams a chance. If you don't succeed that's fine. At least you tried.

- **Dreams Are Free:** You need money to live not the other way around. Be clear about your motives. Prosperity should not define a dream.

- **To See Or Not To See:** Don't get distracted when you have a calling from God. He requires your utmost attention. Stay focused on what you need to do to get the job done.

- **Better Yourself:** Your dreams are a gift from God. He expects the best out of you. Practice good habits, eliminating harmful evils. Learning is a lifelong process.

- **It's You, Not Him:** Blaming God for your problems will not help your dreams succeed. Bad things happen to all of us. In the end, life is what you make of it.

- **Take Time To Make Time:** God is an integral part of life. You cannot hear His voice without spending time with Him. If you long for direction, then make time for the Lord so He can tell you which way to go.

- **Stay in Touch:** It is not enough to check in with God occasionally. When you lose touch, you lose faith. Dreams cannot grow without God's light.

- **A Dream's Purpose:** When a dream brings you joy, you are fulfilling God's intention. Success is not the result; it is only a bonus.

- **Forget Me Not:** Moving on from loss doesn't mean forgetting a loved one. We each have a road to walk, a journey to fulfill.

- **It's All A Test:** Struggle is part of life. God wants to make sure you are awake. He wants you to know that when you get knocked down, you can rise again.

- **A Child Shall Lead Them:** Don't misplace that childlike sense of hope. When things look discouraging, have faith that everything will work out.

- **Choose The Middle One:** Be cautious not to spend too much time in the past or to proceed too far into the future. Neither one exists. All you have is the present.

- **Beware Your Thoughts:** Believing yourself a failure will have disastrous results. Fill your mind with positive messages. You will fare much better when negativity is eliminated.

- **Stay Real:** Every dream is a gift. Humble yourself by using your dreams to honor God.

- **Thanksgiving Is Not Just A Holiday:** Give thanks for the little things in life. Everything is a blessing from God.

- **A Cup of Ambition:** Use ambition to power your dreams but keep it on a leash. If it gets ahead of you, it will drag you to places you have no business being.

- **Follow The Leader:** Mentors are an important part of our earthbound journey. But the one true mentor is God. He is the one to whom you should seek true guidance.

- **Age Is Only A Number:** There are no age restrictions on dreams. If you dream it, go for it.

- **Get Serious:** Show God that you are willing to commit to your dreams. God helps those who help themselves.

- **Grab A Life Jacket:** Life does not always stick to the formula. There are bumps in the road like death, illness, catastrophe, a pandemic. Before you hit the panic button, be still. Ride the waves knowing that God is in control of the boat.

- **Detour Ahead:** Dreams can take a turn. Changing direction does not mean the dream is over. You must be willing to compromise if you expect God to fulfill His end of the bargain.

Afterward

Dear Reader:

Though life is filled with ambiguity, you will conquer mountains you never dreamed possible. The trials you face will come to pass. Pain and sorrow will subside and lead to a stronger you.

You may doubt your capabilities, but God believes differently. He knows that you can do whatever you set your mind to. You are here to learn, to grow. He will guide you as you stumble, reassure you when you are uncertain.

Things may not always be what you expect. There will be times when life's sufferings will test your backbone. Faith will keep you strong, humble, and motivated. As you continue your journey, hold fast to your dreams.

When weakness pursues, show no mercy. You are not alone. God's light eclipses darkness. He wants you to know that He created you for a reason. The only way to discover that reason is to get close to God.

Lastly, reader, life is but for a moment. Use this time to honor God, He whose breath carries you. Keep in mind that whatever you become, you are first and last a child of God. Your allegiance is to Him above all others.

My best to anyone nurturing a dream and to those who are just trying to get by in this life. You are loved and appreciated. God does not make failures, so do the best you can. And no matter what happens, it is OK to dream.

Acknowledgments

Mom and Dad: Thank you for always encouraging me to follow my dreams and for continuing to guide me from above.

Aunt Anna: Thank you for convincing me that I had a calling as a writer and for your unwavering support during your time on this earth. I so appreciate all the letters you sent informing me that it is never too late to follow a dream.

Mentors (teachers, professors): Without your expertise, I wouldn't be where I am today. Your mentorship provided me with insight and inspiration.

Friends: The world would be a lonely place without you. Thank you for always steering me in the right direction and for believing in me when no one else did.

Last but not least, I want to thank God without whom I could do nothing. My dream of being a writer would not have been possible without His thumbprint. I hope to honor Him by using my writing to inspire others and bring them closer to the Lord.

About the Author

Tara Lynn Marta was born in Brooklyn, New York where she lived until moving to Pennsylvania in 1985. She attended Penn State University and earned a B.A. in English and an M.A. in Creative Writing from Wilkes University. Tara was a freelance blogger for *The American Writer's Museum* located in Chicago, IL, and a book reviewer for *At the Inkwell*. Although she has enjoyed success as a fiction writer, she also dabbles in nonfiction and has had several pieces published both online and in print. She is a committee member of Scranton Reads and has moderated several book discussions for local libraries. An avid reader, Tara enjoys classic and contemporary literature. In her spare time, she enjoys hiking, kayaking, and traveling. In addition to being a writer, Tara is also a substitute teacher and motivational speaker. Her first novel *Look Back to Yesterday* was published by Adelaide Books in 2020.

Made in the USA
Columbia, SC
21 October 2021